The Painted Home

The Painted Home

TRANSFORM YOUR HOME WITH COLOR, PATTERN, AND TEXTURE

Kerry Skinner

CRE▲TIVE
HOMEOWNER®

First published in North America in 2005 by

CRE**A**TIVE
HOMEOWNER®

Creative Homeowner® is a registered trademark of
Federal Marketing Corp.

International Standard Book Number: 1-58011-240-4
Library of Congress Catalog Number: 2004113493

QUAR.PHM

Current printing (last digit)
10 9 8 7 6 5 4 3 2 1

Conceived, designed, and produced by
Quarto Publishing plc
The Old Brewery
6 Blundell Street
London N7 9BH

Project Editor Jo Fisher
Art Editors Claire Van Rhyn and Jill Mumford
Designer Karen Raison
Assistant Art Director Penny Cobb
Copy Editor Kathy Steer
Photographer Tim France
Picture Researcher Claudia Tate
Proofreader Alison Howard
Indexer Geraldine Beare

Art Director Moira Clinch
Publisher Piers Spence

Manufactured in Singapore
Printed in Singapore

CREATIVE HOMEOWNER
A Division of Federal Marketing Corp.
24 Park Way
Upper Saddle River, NJ 07458

www.creativehomeowner.com

Contents

Introduction	**6**
Chapter 1: Bold Color	**15**
Lacquered red glaze	**16**
Lapis lazuli washes with flecks of gold	**20**
Sunny yellow ocher	**24**
Variations: Primary colors	**28**
Chapter 2: Color Variations	**31**
Lilac wash over old plaster finish	**32**
Faded and aged green	**36**
Weathered sienna	**40**
Variations: Secondary colors	**44**
Chapter 3: Combining Color	**47**
Violet washes with yellow accents	**48**
Crackled poppy red and spring green	**52**
Orange plaster and blue faux tiles	**56**
Variations: Complementary colors	**60**

Chapter 4: Mixed and Muted — 63
Crimson faux wood effect — 64
Turquoise verdigris — 68
Lime green washes — 72
Variations: Tertiary colors — 76

Chapter 5: Natural Color & Texture — 79
Rusted iron effect — 80
Suede effect panels — 84
Stone effect fire surround — 88
Variations: Natural colors — 92

Chapter 6: Monochromatic Style — 95
Blue-gray geometric panel — 96
Pink and off-white Swedish style — 100
Eggplant frottage — 104
Variations: One-color schemes — 108

Chapter 7: Living with Pattern — 111
Green leaf stencil over pale yellow — 112
Green and blue stripes — 116
Red and orange plaster effect — 120
Variations: Pattern — 124

Glossary — 126
Index — 127
Acknowledgments — 128

Introduction: Understanding Color

This book introduces a variety of paint and plaster effects to demonstrate the atmospheric use of color in your home. Arranged according to basic color theory, a series of decorating schemes will enable you to master a range of easy-to-follow techniques.

Before you begin work on a scheme, it's important to be clear as to your desired final result. Spend some time on planning and organization; collect photographs, other images, and objects, and lay them out together to assess the roles that scale, light, and mood will play in your scheme. Often one object may become the inspiration point for a whole room. Experiment with different lighting to explore the appropriate mood and atmosphere. Furniture, curtains, flooring, and accessories can all be coordinated to complete a scheme.

Everyone has his or her own unique style; there is no prescribed method to achieve the perfect paint effect. The schemes here are offered as a starting point to help you accomplish the particular effect you envisage. But don't be afraid to continue with experiments of your own—a unique, individual painted surface is something to be enjoyed, even loved!

Color Theory

To work successfully with color, you must understand some basic color theory; this teaches you how to influence and create mood and atmosphere.

The most essential point to understand is the difference between the way we perceive a color and how the color we choose is actually mixed with pigments. This involves some level of understanding of the properties of light and the visible color spectrum. Sir Isaac Newton's experiments showed that light, when passed through

This eye-catching interior makes full use of the three primary colors of pigments: red, yellow, and blue.

a prism, breaks up into red, orange, yellow, green, blue, indigo, and violet. These light waves are the visible components of light—known as the visible light spectrum—and each has a different wavelength. This information is transmitted to our brain by our eyes to make it possible to perceive color.

Paint chips

Red, yellow, and blue: the primary colors of pigments.

We see color only when light hits a surface that absorbs certain wavelengths while reflecting others. We see a red surface because that surface reflects the red light waves and absorbs all the others. It is the different combinations of absorbed and reflected light waves that enable us to see different colors.

The result of combining different colored light waves is very different from the result of mixing different colored pigments together. The mixing of light waves is called additive mixing, and the mixing of pigments is known as subtractive mixing. Even the divisions of color into a useful color wheel vary in both cases. The primary colors are those colors that cannot be made by mixing together other colors. (See the Color Wheel right.) The three primary colors of light are red, blue, and green, and these are mixed together to make secondary colors. Red is mixed with blue to make magenta, green and blue are mixed together to make cyan, and green is mixed with red to make yellow. All of these secondary colors are brighter than their constituent primary colors. The primary colors of pigments are red, yellow, and blue. Red is mixed with yellow to make orange, yellow and blue make green, and blue and red make violet. These secondary colors are darker than their constituent primaries.

Try some simple visual experiments of your own. With an understanding of the logic of color theory and an appreciation of the relationship between colors and their combinations, you can choose colors to stimulate, soothe, or enhance. Learning these simple rules enables you to adapt, interpret, and even break them to suit your own aims.

Useful Terms

PRIMARY COLORS

Red, blue, and yellow are called primary colors and are known as the "first" or "principal" colors. They cannot be made by mixing together other colors, and there are several different versions of each. These primary colors are used to mix all the other colors.

SECONDARY COLORS

These are achieved by mixing any two of the primaries. Red and yellow make orange, yellow and blue make green, and blue and red make violet. Different versions of the primaries will create slightly different secondary colors; with the ever-increasing range of synthetic products, endless mixes are available.

TERTIARY COLORS

Also known as "intermediate" colors, these are made by mixing equal amounts of primary and adjacent secondary colors together. For example, red and violet make crimson, blue and green produce turquoise, and yellow and green create lime.

HARMONIOUS COLORS

Harmonious or analogous colors sit next to each other on the color wheel and, when used together, produce calm and restful schemes, as their name suggests. They are close in character—for example, red and orange, blue and green, and green and yellow.

COLOR WHEEL

The color wheel is an invaluable tool. The bands of color—red, orange, yellow, green, blue, and violet—are arranged in a segmented circle to show their relationships. Use it to understand the concept of the primary, secondary, and tertiary colors, as well as complementary and harmonious color juxtapositions.

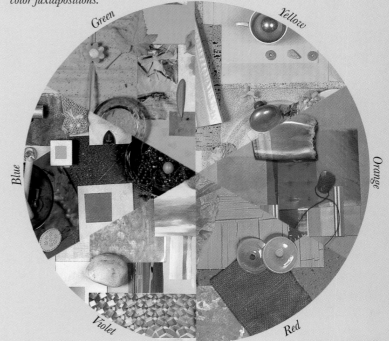

More terms on page 8

This predominantly green scheme is balanced by highlights of red, the complementary color to green.

COMPLEMENTARY COLORS

Complementary colors sit opposite each other on the color wheel. They are called complementary pairs and have a special relationship with one another. Examples are red and green, or orange and blue. Placed side by side, they intensify one another. Combined complementary colors can be very busy and distracting. However, using a small amount of a contrasting color within a one-color scheme is a simple way of achieving an interesting balance.

NEUTRAL COLOR COMBINATIONS

Combining neutral colors, such as black and white, black and yellow, or clashing primaries against white or black will create a dramatic effect.

MONOCHROMATIC

This refers to one-color schemes, or schemes put together from predominantly pastels or other colors tinted with white to result in similar tonal values. Monochromatic schemes produce a very soothing and subtle effect, allowing experimentation with texture and form.

Defining Color

A particular color can be defined by referring to its three qualities: hue, value, and intensity.

HUE

Hue is the specific spectral name of a color, such as red, yellow, or blue. The color "pink" for instance is a red hue.

VALUE

Value refers to the darkness or lightness of the color; this includes tints, shades, and tones. Tints are created by adding white, and shades are made by adding black. A sense of tone can easily be gained from the color wheel, where yellow has the brightest tone and violet the darkest. Red and green have a similar tonal value, which helps to explain why some people suffering from red/green color blindness cannot define the two colors.

INTENSITY

Intensity refers to the saturation of color—its purity and brightness. A color with high intensity is bright, strong, and clean, as opposed to one that is muted, dirty, or dull.

Warm and Cool Colors

Paint swatches showing different red values

Colors are described as being either warm or cool; the color wheel has both a warm and a cool side (see page 7). The warm side comprises the reds, oranges, and yellows, while the cool side is made up of the greens, violets, and blues. These colors can elicit an emotional response. Red is associated with passion, and blue suggests space, coolness, and tranquility.

Light Effects and Texture

Consider the effects of light and texture when planning a project. For example, the textural finish of an applied color will affect its appearance. A matte or rough surface will seem darker than a shiny, glossy one due to the difference in reflected light. Think about the source and quality of light available. View paint samples in both daylight and artificial light to examine how the color changes. Mirrors, glass, and metal can all be used to reflect and diffuse color and light. Choose paint carefully; the choice will depend on the area you wish to decorate. Smooth, easy-to-wipe painted surfaces will be more appropriate for a kitchen, while textural finishes are better in an area where you want to suggest softness and comfort, such as in a bedroom or reception room.

Color and Mood

Color evokes a range of feeling as described here. Creating a mood, or sample, board is an excellent way to begin planning a scheme.

RED ▼

Representing warmth, confidence, and boldness, all reds inject vitality and energy into a scheme. The richness of deep reds, warm browns, and dark pinks offers a striking appearance and welcoming atmosphere. Pinks and oranges add an unusual but warming touch to any effect.

BLUE ▶

Blues are universally loved; shades of sky and sea inspire the soothing calmness of the elements. Blues combined together or with other colors are almost always successful in a scheme.

PATTERN AND TEXTURE ▼

The use of pattern and texture always adds a distinct character to a color scheme. Discover and experiment with the huge array of patterns and textures found in nature. Close investigation of the weave of a fabric or the density and variation in a piece of stone or wood will offer a surprising amount of detail.

YELLOW ▲

Yellows suggest spring and summer, growth, sunshine, and vitality. A particularly happy color to work with, yellow introduces energy and a sense of wellbeing. From pastel creams and acid lemon yellow, to bright and bold cadmium and chrome yellows, each offers a different character to a room.

Tools and Equipment

One of the secrets of success in decorative painting is to have the correct tool for the job. Always buy the best tools you can afford. They will pay for themselves in the end, especially if you care for them properly.

SPONGES

Sponges are used for colorwashing, stippling, and cleaning. A prepared decorator's sponge is ideal for colorwashing. Made from cellulose, these have a similar texture to natural sponges but are cheaper to buy. To prepare the sponge for use, rinse it in water and detergent to remove any yellow dye and let it dry. Cut it in half with a sharp knife. Trim around the heat-sealed edges, and tear off the outer sides. Pick off pieces around the edges and corners to give an irregular shape similar to a natural sponge.

Sponges

ROLLERS

Rollers are used to apply base colors, textured effects, and bands of colors. The many types of roller heads available include foam, textured, and sheepskin. Small-headed radiator rollers are used to reach inaccessible places and are perfect for painting stripes.

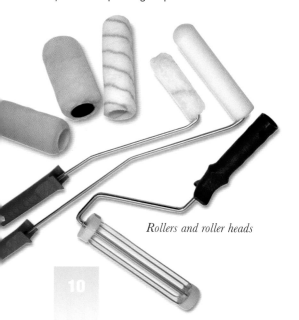

Rollers and roller heads

PAINTS

Most of the paints used here are chosen because they are more environmentally friendly; they contain organic pigments, binders, and solvents wherever possible. Buy only the amount of paint necessary for each scheme.

Tubes of acrylic paint can be used to paint large areas if they are diluted with some water and glaze. Color stainers are concentrated coloring agents, which can be added to cans of white flat latex paint so you can mix the color you desire. There is a huge range of types of paint available today, and the list that follows describes those most commonly encountered.

Acrylic primer is water-based and is used for sealing and preparing surfaces for decorating.

Oil-based primer and undercoat can be used to seal and prime most surfaces. It is available in many different colors, such as red oxide, gray, white, black, and brown.

BRUSHES

A wide range of brushes is available from home improvement stores.

Decorators' paintbrushes are available in a range of sizes. Choose a straight-edge brush for priming and undercoating and a chisel-edge brush for cutting in edges. Use the size with which you feel comfortable and which is most suitable for the job.

Decorators' paintbrushes

Fitch brushes are usually made of hog hair and are used for mixing small quantities of paint and painting fine lines and difficult-to-reach edges and corners.

Wire brushes are used for preparing and cleaning surfaces and for liming techniques.

Real bristle nailbrushes are used to spatter drops of color.

Varnishing brushes come in various sizes. They can be flat or domed. It is very difficult to load too much varnish onto the brush.

Artists' brushes are available in a variety of sizes and lengths. They are used for mixing small amounts of color as well as adding fine detail and working in tight corners. A fine artists' brush can be used instead of a lining brush.

Dragging brushes are long-bristled brushes that are used for dragging and graining techniques.

Softening brushes, such as those made from high-quality badger hair, are expensive. A cheaper option is either a hog hair softener or a dusting brush, which can also be used to remove dust.

Stencil brushes come in various sizes. They can be either domed or flat and produce a fine stipple effect when used over a stencil.

Acrylic paints in pots and tubes

Latex paint (water-based) is available in flat, eggshell, satin, semigloss, and gloss finishes.

Stencil paint is water-based and generally flows much better than latex paint. It is available in metallic and glitter colors and can also be used as a stainer.

Wood paint is a flat, opaque paint specially formulated for wood. It is self-priming, has a high chalk and pigment content, and can be diluted with water to create a wash for bare wood.

Oil-based paint is available in gloss, semi-gloss, satin, and eggshell (semi-matte) finishes. Gloss is used as a finishing coat on woodwork. Satin and eggshell are used on woodwork and on walls wherever general wear and tear is likely. They are all scrubbable.

Acrylic eggshell paint is a more user-friendly version of eggshell oil-based paint, with a lot less odor.

Metallic paints are widely available in tubes, pots, powder form, and spray cans. New acrylic products are also available in a range of iridescent, opalescent, and interference colors. These shimmering effects are quite transparent.

Colorwash is a specially formulated, water-based, translucent, colored glaze containing glycol retardants.

Artists' oil paints are used for tinting oil glazes for broken-color work and oil-based marbling effects. You could use universal tinters as a more economic alternative to artists' oil paints.

Alternative plasters such as stucco or marmorino are available for those with more specialized knowledge and an understanding of their application. The finish is harder and can be polished to give a smooth, soft gleam.

Textured paint is available commercially, but texture additives are also available in powder form. They are a mix of quartz, clays, and cellulose, and can be added to flat latex paint by the spoonful.

To make your own textured paint
Add approximately 1 part paint-texturing powder to 2 parts paint. It is best to mix the powder in a little water before adding it to the paint to achieve a creamy consistency. Allow a sample of the mix to dry to check its true color.

Always wear protective gloves when mixing and working with textured paint, and always follow the manufacturer's instructions.

Texturing powder

Liquid solvents for thinning

THINNERS

For water-based and acrylic products, use water for thinning and cleaning while still wet.

For oil-based products, use liquid solvent or linseed oil for thinning. Use liquid solvent for cleaning, and use paint stripper for removing paint from surfaces.

PROTECTIVE FINISHES

Oil-based varnish is more robust than its water-based equivalent, but may yellow with age.

Resin-based water-soluble varnish does not yellow, is reasonably heat- and water-resistant, and is more user-friendly. It is available in matte or satin.

Acrylic water-based polyurethane is quick drying and available in matte, semigloss, or gloss finish.

Acrylic glaze is non-yellowing and heat- and water-resistant. It can be tinted with universal stainers and acrylic paints for decorative glaze work. Water-based, it has a short working time, about 15 to 20 minutes.

Matte latex glaze is water-based and is used to thin color and to act as a protective top coat sealant.

Transparent oil glaze is available in matte, satin, and gloss finishes. It is used for oil-based glazing paint effects but tends to yellow with age.

Varnishes and glazes for protecting painted surfaces

WAXES

Beeswax is a traditional wax used to prevent wood from drying out. It is available in liquid form (applied with a brush) and in a paste form (applied with a lint-free cloth).

Liming wax imitates bleached wood by leaving a film of white in the grain and so works best on open-grained woods.

Colored wax or furniture wax comes in easily applicable forms and in varying colors.

Waxes

OTHER MATERIALS

Metallic or opalescent shimmer and bronze powders are available in many different guises. They are usually water-based or come as a dry powder, mixed by hand. Always follow the manufacturer's instructions.

ALL-PURPOSE FILLERS

All-purpose fillers are used to fill and prepare surfaces for priming and can be used to thicken paint for textured effects. They are available in powdered and ready-made forms.

HEALTH AND SAFETY

Always wear a dust mask or respirator and protective gloves when working with oil- and alcohol-based paints, plasters, powders, varnishes, waxes, and other products. If you have sensitive skin, also wear gloves when using water-based products because lengthy exposure can dry your skin out.

When sanding or using toxic products, wear a dust mask and goggles to protect your eyes and lungs.

Always work in a well-ventilated area.

When working up a ladder, make sure that your feet are solidly positioned and will not slip and that the braces are securely locked down. Never try to extend beyond comfortable reach, as the ladder could tip over.

Remember to protect all surfaces with dust covers to prevent possible damage.

Do not throw rags soaked in volatile liquids such as liquid solvent directly into the trash can. Lay them out flat to dry before discarding them.

Label all containers clearly, and keep paints and chemicals out of the reach of children.

Whatever product you are using, always read and follow the manufacturer's instructions.

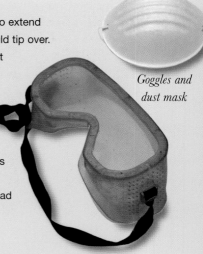

Goggles and dust mask

OTHER USEFUL TOOLS

Heart graining tools are used for wood-graining finishes. They are usually made of rubber and come in different widths and grades.

Plasterers' hawk and float are used for applying plaster.

Spirit level marks out accurate horizontal lines.

Plumb line (chalkline) gives perfect vertical lines.

Pencil, **eraser, and chalk** are used for marking.

Ruler, steel ruler, straightedge, and measuring tape are used for measuring and marking.

Plastic containers are necessary for pouring out paint into usable amounts and for mixing paints and plasters. Paint buckets and roller trays are available in metal or plastic.

Lint-free cloths are useful for wiping down and removing dust from surfaces as well as for applying waxes, polishing, removing mistakes, cleaning up spills, and wiping your brushes. You can use old clean clothes, but make sure they are made from absorbent natural fibers that will not shed during use.

Graph, tracing, stencil paper, and cardstock are all available from art supply stores.

Cardstock can be purchased in various thicknesses and can be used for sample boards or for textured paint.

Stencil paper is flexible and strong. An alternative is to use transparent stencil acetate. Always use a mat board.

Sharp scissors, craft knife, or scalpel is used for cutting straight edges and stencils.

Masking tape is available in various sizes and levels of adhesive. Low-tack masking tape is ideal for use over newly painted surfaces.

Mat board with wood and rubber stamp, steel ruler, transparent stencil acetate, scalpel, and scissors

Scrapers are essential for stripping paint and varnish and for cleaning up flaking areas. They are also useful for filling cracks and holes and using ready-made fillers.

Wire wool comes in different grades and is used for preparing surfaces. Fine wire wool can be used to apply wax, smooth a surface, and lightly lift off a top coat to reveal base colors.

Sandpaper comes in a selection of grades. Wet-and-dry sandpaper is more expensive but lasts longer and is more easily controlled.

Everyday household items are always handy: a screwdriver to open paint cans; a spoon to measure powders and pigments; a whisk to mix paint and plasters.

CHAPTER 1

Bold Color

INTRODUCE THE THREE PRIMARY COLORS, RED, YELLOW, AND BLUE, SUCCESSFULLY INTO YOUR HOME.

The primary colors provide bold and immediate statements, yet the schemes here show that, with some planning, you may create a peaceful and beautiful environment. It is important to understand the relationship between our perceptions of color and how the color we choose is mixed. See pages 6-9 for a discussion of the properties of light and the visible color spectrum.

The first scheme shows you how to use red successfully, achieving subtlety and variation by building up thin layers of glaze. The second scheme introduces a faux paint effect inspired by lapis lazuli, with subtle coloration and interesting flecks and veins of gold. The lime-washed room in the third scheme demonstrates the warmth and conviviality yellow can bring to a home and introduces texturing as a way of manipulating light effects.

A brush is used to build up a rich glowing depth of color in layers followed by a soft buffed wax finish. Consider the intensity of the red and the use of the room in which it will appear—it may be perfect for a dining room or an accent wall.

Lacquered red glaze

This painting technique may appear rather labor intensive, but if the end result is compared with a wall painted in a flat red paint, the glazed wall will display more obvious depth and luminosity, offering a luxurious appearance. The built-up layers give a smooth, sensual warmth, especially when finished with layers of buffed beeswax sealant. Try out the color on a sample board to decide the depth of color, first, because you cannot lighten the red halfway through the project.

Preparation is very important. The surface must be as smooth as silk with no holes, cracks, or textures to interfere with the application of the red glazes. The highest quality finish can be achieved by completing the effect in oil-based glazes over a perfect gesso or eggshell paint, but because of the prolonged drying time water-based paints are recommended for large areas. Furniture or small accent areas can be done following the same technique using oil-based paints.

YOU WILL NEED

For preparation
- All-purpose filler
- Acrylic primer
- Fine- and medium-grade wet-and-dry sandpaper

For base color
- Pale pink acrylic eggshell paint
- Foam roller and tray
- Plastic strainer

For painting
- Light red (cadmium) acrylic paint
- Deep red (alizarin crimson) acrylic gloss paint
- Acrylic glaze
- Protective gloves
- Decorators' paintbrushes
- Cellulose decorators' sponge
- Paint buckets
- Fine-grade wet-and-dry sandpaper
- Beeswax
- Lint-free soft cloth or tack cloth

MOOD BOARD

The reflective red surfaces of a collection of small metal tins and lacquered boxes inspired imitation. The pattern in the mini Turkish rug and some natural wood paneling add to the sense of luxury.

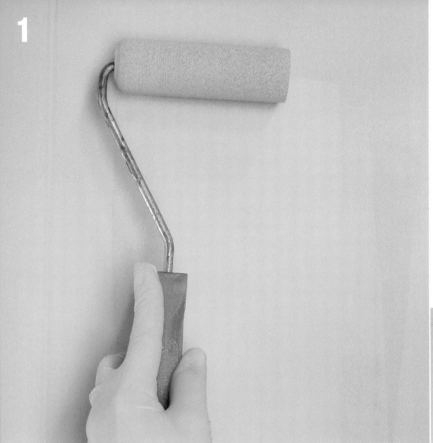

1 PREPARING THE SURFACE
Fill any holes or cracks with all-purpose filler and, once dry, sand until smooth. Apply a coat of acrylic primer and, when dry, sand until as smooth as possible. Thoroughly mix the base coat to make sure that there are no lumps, then carefully apply the base coat with a foam roller. Use the roller in all directions to achieve an even finish.

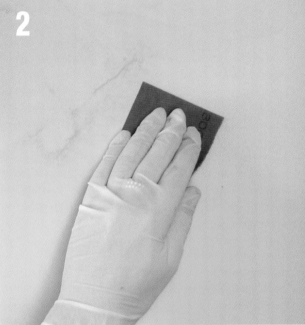

2 APPLYING THE BASE COLOR
When the eggshell paint is completely dry, lightly sand the surface with fine wet-and-dry sandpaper, using a circular motion, until smooth. Repeat with at least one more coat of eggshell paint and lightly sand after each layer. It may be necessary to build up layers of up to four coats of paint to achieve a good enough finish for the colorwashing.

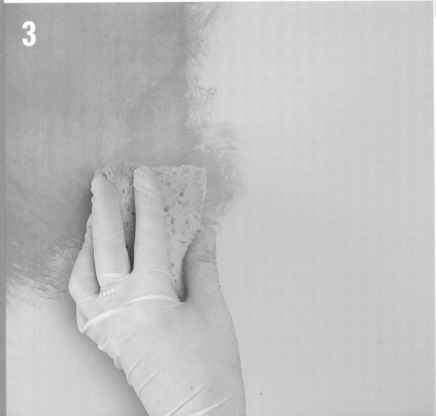

3 PAINTING
Dilute the light red paint with acrylic glaze in a 50:50 ratio, and add a splash of water. Dampen the sponge and use a brush to load it with the glaze mix. Use a brush to reach more awkward areas and wipe with a sponge to avoid obvious brush marks. Begin at an edge and, using quick circular movements sponge the glaze over an area about 2 ft square. Reload the sponge and go over another area nearby. To join up the two areas, flip over the sponge and soften the two patches so the join is feathered in with a more dilute area. This will help to avoid darker edges where the areas meet up. Let dry completely.

4 To eliminate any build-up of unsightly heavy join marks, always begin the next layer in a different area. The meeting of each new glazed patch of paint should be treated as described in Step 3. Flip over the sponge to the clean side and feather out the glaze to meet the next patch. Work quickly and smoothly over the whole wall. It may be better to work with a partner but swap positions frequently to avoid any inconsistency because everyone works using a slightly different pressure. Let dry between each coat.

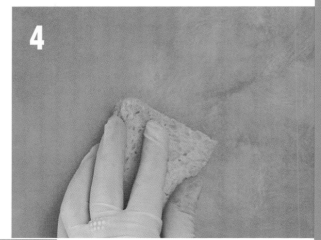

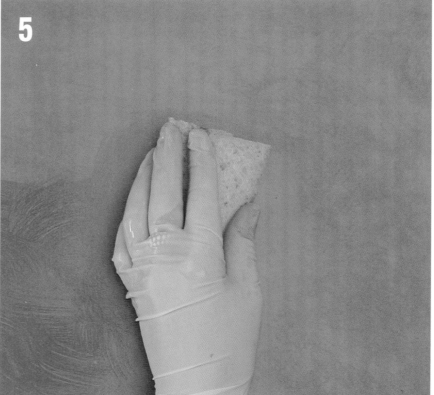

5 Always clean the sponge and brush regularly in soapy water. Dilute the deep-red paint with water in a 2:3 ratio to achieve a creamy consistency. Lightly and evenly wash this mix over the surface. Keep changing the area of the patches so the meeting edges move around, preventing any patterns or shapes from standing out. Let dry. Lightly sand the surface with very fine wet-and-dry sandpaper before the final coat to remove any dust.

6 FINISHING
Wipe over the whole surface with beeswax and buff it with a lint-free soft cloth. Repeat if necessary. If the lacquer effect has been applied to furniture, varnish it first, then wax the finish. Apply at least two alternating coats of varnish and wax and lightly sand between layers when each is completely dry.

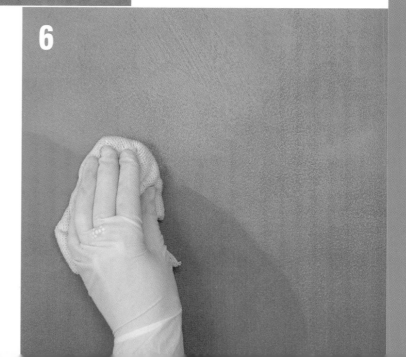

BOLD COLOR

The wonderful clear blue pigment created by the mineral lapis lazuli remains an inspiration for many faux finishes. Washes of sponged-on thin paint build up a unique velvety blue color, which is highlighted with a gold starlike spatter.

Lapis lazuli washes with flecks of gold

The blue panel in this scheme is achieved by washing on layers of dilute ultramarine blue acrylic paint and ultramarine with a touch of burnt umber to slightly deepen some areas. Applying the paint in layers adds strength and luminosity because the glaze hardens and adheres to the surface much better than thick, flat paint. A thin, protective layer of clear wax, buffed with a cloth to give a soft sheen, has also been applied. If the paint effect is applied to a surface which may be subjected to wear and tear, varnish it with a satin varnish.

It is crucial to prepare the surface well so that the washed-over layers build up with little texture or marking. The texture is added at the end with a light spattering of blues, a little burnt umber, and then gold paint. A painted panel or canvas is a simple and contemporary way to add a strong splash of color to any scheme without having to commit to a complete color change.

YOU WILL NEED:

For preparation
- All-purpose filler
- White acrylic primer
- Medium-grade wet-and-dry sandpaper
- Fine foam roller and tray

For base color
- Pale blue acrylic eggshell paint

For painting
- Ultramarine acrylic paint
- Burnt umber acrylic paint
- White latex paint
- Bright gold metallic acrylic paint
- Protective gloves
- Decorators' paintbrushes
- Cellulose decorators' sponge
- Paint buckets
- Fine-grade wet-and-dry sandpaper
- Real bristle nailbrush
- Beeswax
- Lint-free soft cloth or tack cloth

MOOD BOARD

Neutrals and strong metallic colors balance the intense pattern and texturing of a piece of unpolished lapis lazuli stone. The simple geometric appearance of the sample board will be reflected in the room.

1 PREPARING THE SURFACE

Fill any holes or cracks with all-purpose filler. When dry, sand until smooth and brush off any loose dust and particles. Dilute the acrylic primer with water in a 1:1 ratio and brush a thin coat over the surface. When dry, apply the base coat with a fine foam roller to give a smooth finish.

2 BUILDING UP THE BASE COLOR

When the eggshell paint is completely dry, lightly sand the surface with fine-grade wet-and-dry sandpaper until smooth. Build the layers with up to three coats of paint for a smooth, solid surface. Each layer of paint should be applied in a different direction to achieve an even finish.

3 PAINTING

Make a glaze mix of acrylic ultramarine paint and water in a 1:3 ratio. Dampen a sponge and use a brush to load it with the glaze mix. Wipe the surface using a figure eight movement and repeatedly wash over the glaze to create a cloud-like effect. Re-wipe the layers as they dry to reduce any marks. Wipe the edges of the panel and blend in any excess. Let dry; then repeat until the required depth of color is achieved. The layers will become easier and quicker to blend as the base paint becomes more saturated. Always wipe until dry otherwise any wet paint will leave a darker patch.

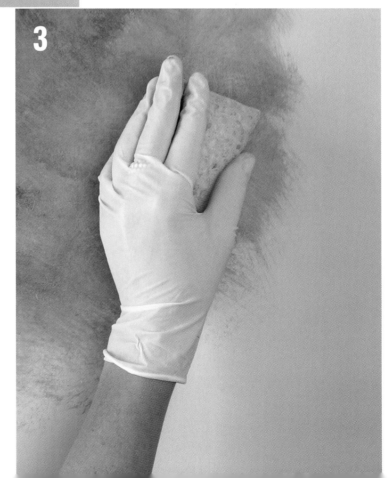

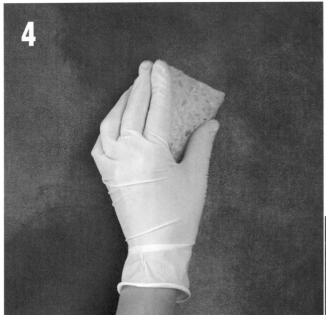

4 Apply darker blue clouds in some areas to add depth and interest. Slightly darken the glaze mix with burnt umber acrylic paint in a 4:1 ratio and add a little extra water. Wash as in Step 3 and apply at least two layers. Let dry; then add another layer of the original ultramarine glaze to unify the final finish. Let dry.

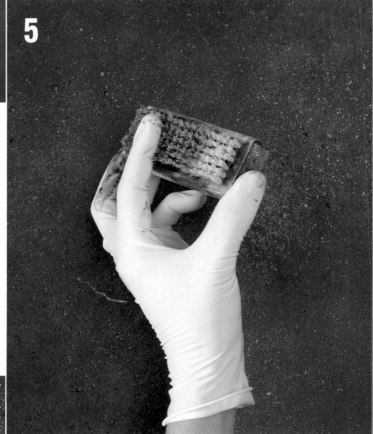

5 ADDING TEXTURE
Make a new mix of ultramarine glaze with a touch of white in a 4:1 ratio and spatter the surface to create a fine texture. Concentrate on areas you wish to have a lighter contrast to the main blue. Let dry; then repeat with the ultramarine and burnt umber glaze as before. To achieve a more consistent spatter, pull your finger across a bristle nailbrush, which has been lightly loaded with paint. Let dry.

6 FINISHING
Apply random spatters of bright gold acrylic paint using the same method as in Step 5. Always make sure the nailbrush is thoroughly cleaned with warm, soapy water and dried completely between color changes. Overloading the brush could result in drops and large splotches of paint, which could spoil the effect. It is best to apply lightly, then let dry and add more if required. Let dry overnight; then protect the panel from damage or marking with a thin coat of beeswax applied with a lint-free cloth and buffed to a soft sheen.

A lime-based paint in a warm yellow ocher is painted on the walls over a lime-compatible off-white latex paint. The slightly antiqued or dulled appearance of the yellow is soft on the eye and easy to live with.

Sunny yellow ocher

This technique is most suitable for old plaster walls, which may otherwise require stripping, sealing, and re-painting. If completing new construction, however, you can add the paint as the finishing touch to walls made from plaster, wallboard, brick, stucco, or stone. Only pigments that can tolerate lime should be added to colored lime-based paints, the most successful being natural earth pigments. The mixes are available on the internet, but it is possible to create your own paint following the recipe guide on page 11. Keep a record of quantities used and always mix enough for each coat. Be prepared for color variations, which add to the unique quality of the finish. The best final results are achieved with up to four coats of the lime-based paint. Vary the appearance further by diluting the mix with more water and adding a final layer onto the previous coat of paint when completely dry to give a lighter topcoat. The finish will demonstrate the effect of light, reflecting a chalky or satin finish as the light catches the brush strokes.

YOU WILL NEED

For preparation
- All-purpose filler
- Off-white lime-compatible flat latex paint
- Sheepskin roller and tray
- Medium-grade wet-and-dry sandpaper

For painting
- Deep yellow ocher lime-based earth paint
- Protective gloves
- Decorators' paintbrushes
- Paint buckets
- Goggles
- Face mask
- Newspaper for cleaning up waste materials

MOOD BOARD
Photographs of worn and textured walls in different shades of yellow ranging from pale cream to warm ocher, together with a selection of yellow flowers, have inspired this scheme.

1 PREPARING THE SURFACE
Fill any holes or cracks with all-purpose filler. When dry, sand until smooth and brush off any old paint and loose particles. Apply two coats of flat finish off-white latex paint with a roller and paintbrush. Let dry.

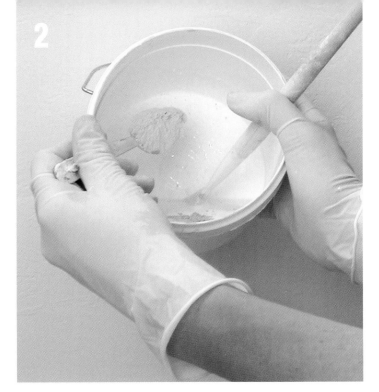

2 MIXING THE PAINT

Follow the manufacturer's instructions to mix correct quantities of the lime-based paint. Stir in small quantities of powder until all the pigment is absorbed evenly into the lime and water to the consistency of thick cream. Wear protective gloves, goggles, and face mask when working with lime products and powder pigments. The powder can be an irritant to the respiratory system and skin. If any contact occurs, rinse immediately with water. Always keep products and containers safely away from children and animals. Do not empty any remaining paint into drains or water courses. Clean and empty into old newspaper and rinse brushes in a bucket of water. Pour any residual waste into newspapers after letting the bucket's contents settle to the bottom. The water can be poured off into the sink.

3 Using a paintbrush, dampen the surface of the wall with water. This helps with the application of the paint. If working over a large area, dampen the area to be painted just before application.

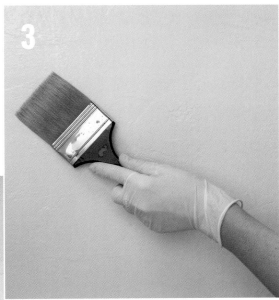

4 PAINTING

Begin painting immediately, using a medium-size paintbrush. Do not overload the brush with paint and try to keep the layer as even as possible. Avoid applying the paint too thickly or it will craze and flake off when dry. Always apply one full coat to the wall because any retouching of isolated patches will show. Brush the paint in different directions to make it as even as possible. Let dry overnight. The paint will dry to a lighter color and will also change from a translucent appearance to opaque when dry.

SUNNY YELLOW OCHER 25

5

5 To achieve the best result, apply additional coats of paint. If you have enough of the first batch left, continue with a second layer after dampening the wall again. If you must mix another batch, be aware that the color may vary slightly. Let dry.

6

6 If some areas have become slightly too textured, lightly rub down the surface with wet-and-dry sandpaper. Always protect your skin from the effects of the lime paint and do not breathe in the dust. Always wear goggles and a face mask.

7

7 For variation to the overall finish, introduce lighter areas here and there. Dilute the mix with water and apply it randomly without dampening the wall. Smooth out the highlights by feathering the edges, softening the graduation from dark to light.

BOLD COLOR

Primary colors

The vibrancy and richness of the primary colors may be enhanced with a range of different techniques. Here, red is given a polished plaster finish, while blue is finished with ultrafine marble plaster. Layers of colorwash are built up to produce two different deep, lustrous tones of yellow.

◄ RED PLASTER EFFECT

This variation resembles the technique used in the red and orange plaster effect scheme. (See page 120.) Add a stronger red pigment to the plaster, and apply to the surface in layers. Finally, polish to a shine. Use lime-compatible pigments to achieve good results.

STUCCO PLASTER FINISH ►

In another variation to the red and orange plaster effect scheme, add blue colorant to the lime plaster. Apply a top coat of fine marble (also known as stucco lustro, the finest of the lime and marble dust plasters available) after the first two coats of marmorino have nearly dried.

Stucco plaster comes ready-mixed in pots. You can buy it already colored or add your own pigment. Apply it with either a steel trowel or a continental filling knife. Build up layers until you achieve the required depth of color and texture.

Work each layer over the previous one while it's still damp. Apply the layers in a continuous motion, pulling at and wiping the plaster, and repeatedly changing direction. As the surface becomes more solid, begin to polish by lowering the angle of the trowel or knife and gently pulling it in all directions over the surface as it dries, to give a glossy sheen.

◄ YELLOW OCHER COLORWASH

The lacquered red glaze scheme inspired this variation. (See page 16.) Build up thin layers of yellow ocher acrylic paint in figure eight movements, followed by a soft buffed waxed finish to produce a good, solid depth of color.

YELLOW AND WHITE COLORWASH OVER PALE CREAM BASE COLOR ►

Again, a similar technique to that used in the lacquered red glaze scheme is applied here. Apply the pale cream base coat, and leave it to dry, then, using a sponge, apply a coat of yellow acrylic paint diluted with a little water to the surface. Mix the yellow acrylic paint with some white latex paint in a 2:1 ratio to soften the color, and then apply to the surface. Let dry. Add further layers of paint diluted with white until you achieve the desired effect.

VARIATIONS

CHAPTER 2

Color Variations

EXPLORE THE RICHNESS OF THE SECONDARY COLORS: LILAC, GREEN, AND ORANGE.

Each of the effects in this chapter is achieved using a different method of layering color to develop varying intensities of tone and texture. The techniques can be applied to most surfaces and demonstrate three ways to create variation and movement to express the potential of the colors.

The lilac wash scheme shown first enhances the shape of the recessed window, and the layers of pink and blue are perfectly suited to the textured surface of the old plaster wall. The second technique, the aged green effect, is applied to tongue-and-groove paneling in a bathroom. The green is blended from light to dark along the vertical grooves, giving the room movement and life. The last scheme in this section adds interest to a passageway; it links the inside with the outside by suggesting the natural aging of an outdoor wall.

Here is a tried-and-true method for giving extra interest to a simple recessed window. The addition of the painted band around the window makes an unusual feature and offers the opportunity to add color without dominating the room.

Lilac washes over old plaster finish

This color effect is created by applying alternating layers of pink and blue flat latex paint in a similar tone; the colors combine for a luminous, soft lilac-blue finish. The recessed area is given extra layers of paint to provide depth and intensity of color, while the outer band appears lighter and sun-bleached. The band can be lightly sanded to lend a more lived-in look to the room. This blurs the masked edge, slightly, for a softer, almost powdery finish.

To create the rough-textured surface of the wall, loosely plaster the area with quick drying one-coat plaster, then apply a coat of cream-color flat latex paint. The textured surface allows the diluted color to sink to various levels, producing minute color variations.

YOU WILL NEED

For preparation
- Medium-grade wet-and-dry sandpaper
- Damp cloth

For plastering
- Plasterers' hawk and trowel
- Ready-mixed one-coat plaster

For painting
- Off-white, pink, and pale blue flat latex paint
- Protective gloves
- Deocrators' paintbrushes and/or roller
- Cellulose decorators' sponge
- Paint buckets
- Painters' tape
- Pencil
- Measuring tape
- Steel ruler
- Lint-free soft cloth or tack cloth

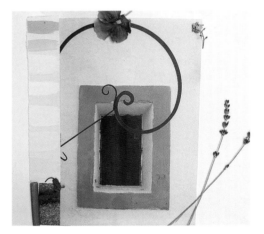

MOOD BOARD

The simple shape and border decoration suggest rusticity, which can be balanced with more sophisticated wrought iron furniture and other floral or checked patterns. Selecting exactly the right cream and lilac to work with needs some care.

1 PREPARING THE SURFACE
Lightly sand the surface clean and wipe it down with a damp cloth to remove any dust and grease.

2 PLASTERING THE AREA
Roughly plaster the surface with a thin application of one-coat white plaster. Let dry thoroughly—this normally takes 24 hours.

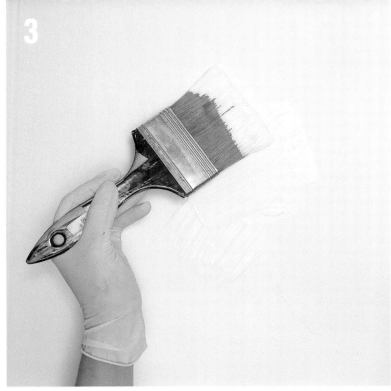

3 PAINTING
When the plaster is completely dry, apply a solid, even coat of off-white flat latex paint to the whole surface using a brush or a roller. Make sure the surface is completely covered and let dry.

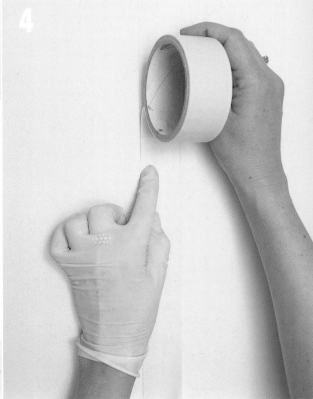

4 Use a pencil and measuring tape to mark a border around the window. Draw the line as carefully as possible along a steel ruler or other straight edge. Mask the edge of the border with painters' tape, burnishing the edge with your fingers. This will prevent the tape from lifting the paint when it is removed.

5 Use a brush to paint the pale blue base color over the masked area and the recessed inner window. You may want to mask the window frame too, although it should be possible to wipe off any excess color on the frame with a damp sponge. Let dry.

LILAC WASHES

6 Choose pink and blue flat latex paint in similar tones and dilute each color 1:1 with water. Load the pink paint on the sponge with a brush so the sponge doesn't become overloaded with color. Apply the paint to the surface with the sponge in regular, firm, circular movements; this will push the color deeper into the recesses of the textured plaster. Use a decorators' paintbrush to apply color to the edges and then lift off the paint slightly giving it a quick wipe over with the sponge. Let dry.

7 Now apply the blue wash in the same way, but this time vary the mix by pushing less of the blue into the recesses while allowing it to sit on the top surface. This lets the full strength of the pink show through in a random pattern. Let dry. Repeat as required, adding more layers to the recessed area and fewer to the outer band. This will leave it lighter in appearance and create the variable depth of color. Let dry.

8 FINISHING
For a softer finish, apply a final layer of the pale blue base color using a damp sponge. Try to allow patches of the deeper colors to show through randomly. Don't work this last layer too heavily or you may obliterate the previous colors. Let dry.

Remove the masking tape and lightly sand the edges of the colorwashed area. The sanding gives more depth and texture to the paint effect because some of the color is lifted and the base colors begin to appear again.

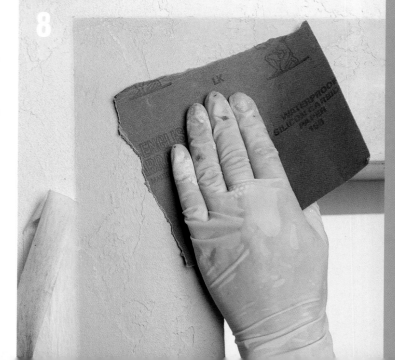

COLOR VARIATIONS

Give interest to a room by applying color in different strengths. Here, tints of blue-green and yellow are added to the bright green main color. The deeper colors are brushed over a pale green base color.

Faded and aged green

Variations in color often occur in nature—on a single leaf or a piece of wood or stone. The faded-green effect achieved here gives the appearance of old wood aged by the sun, the upper part more sun-bleached and worn. The galvanized metal bathtub, hooks, and the reflective old glass of the mirror all show an aging of bright surfaces. Sample boards are essential before starting work. Paint a series of different greens and see how they look at different times of the day and next to other colored fabrics and samples.

Preparation is also important. The woodwork should be cleaned with washing soda to degrease the surface, then sand and prepare with acrylic primer. Then lightly sand it again and apply two coats of acrylic eggshell paint in a pale green color. Lightly sand when dry. Protect the final paint from water damage with two coats of water-based polyurethane. A varnish may be used, but it will alter the color slightly by yellowing over time. The painted floor and bathtub have also been treated with two coats of water-based polyurethane.

YOU WILL NEED

For preparation
- Washing soda
- Acrylic all-purpose primer
- Fine-grade wet-and-dry sandpaper

For the base color
- Pale green acrylic eggshell paint

For painting
- Blue-green, medium green, and light green acrylic and latex paints
- Matte acrylic glaze
- Low-luster water-based polyurethane
- Protective gloves
- Decorators' paintbrushes
- Paint buckets

MOOD BOARD

Observing the effects of aging on an old painted door and the variety of shades of green in leaves and on paint chips has inspired the decoration for this bathroom. The galvanized metal accessories accent the greens.

1 PREPARING THE SURFACE
Clean the woodwork thoroughly using washing soda and brush off any dust and loose particles. Apply a coat of all-purpose primer to the areas that are to be painted. When dry, apply two good coats of pale green eggshell paint as a base color. Let dry between coats and lightly sand the surface with fine wet-and-dry sandpaper after each layer.

2 Mix up three green paints varying in strength: a blue-green, a medium green, and a light green. These greens should be slightly darker than the base color. Add some acrylic glaze to each paint mix in the ratio of 2:1 and a little water. The colors will be quite transparent, so they will need to be applied in more than one layer.

Begin the shading by applying the darkest color first. Brush up from the bottom of the wall to about halfway. Do not bring the color up evenly, but let some boards feather out lower and higher; too neat a line will appear contrived.

3 PAINTING
While the dark color is still wet, use a clean brush and start to introduce the medium green slightly above the darker green. This can be lightly brushed and blended into the dark color.

4 Begin at the top of the woodwork with a clean brush loaded with the light green paint and work it down until it meets the medium green. Blend in before the paint is dry.

5 When the colors have dried, apply the layers again. Start in the center with a quick wash of the medium green color, then adding the darker and lighter shades at the bottom and top before the paint has dried.

6 FINISHING
Enhance the effect by adding some of the base color at the highest point and blending it into the medium green. Repeat the entire process as many times as possible to achieve a solid appearance. Let dry, then lightly sand and apply two coats of water-based polyurethane. The walls above the tongue-and-groove panelling have been brushed over with the darkest green in random cross-hatching and sealed with two coats of varnish. The outside of the bath has been painted in the same way and protected with water-based polyurethane.

This passageway, a functional and utilitarian space, is given a facelift by painting the walls to look like old colored plaster, faded and aged by time and exposure to sunlight and condensation, and with a distinct character.

Weathered sienna

This technique will work on any painted surface and has a unique and individual appearance. Earthy colors can be particularly effective because they emulate the natural weathering process on old plaster or clay walls.

The color used here, burnt sienna over an orange base color, is a natural earth pigment that is diluted in water and mixed with a matte glaze to form a colorwash. The quantity of pigment is varied in the mixes; some are thinner, diluted with more water and glaze, and one is very dark, which is used for the niches and other patches. The whole wall is softened with a thin coat of the pale base color diluted with water, then given two coats of low-luster oil varnish, diluted with some liquid solvent.

MOOD BOARD

Laying together some photographs of old plastered walls, clay pots, painted samples of textured paint effects, and limestone flag stones demonstrates how different terracotta, orange, and apricot colors may be effectively combined.

YOU WILL NEED

For preparation
- Washing soda
- Pale terracotta flat latex paint
- Roller and tray
- Wet-and-dry sandpaper

For base color
- Burnt sienna pigment
- Matte glaze

For painting
- Low-luster oil varnish
- Liquid solvent
- Protective gloves
- Decorators' paintbrushes
- Cellulose decorators' sponge
- Paint buckets

1 PREPARING THE SURFACE
Clean the walls with washing soda and brush off any dust and loose particles. Using a roller in all directions, apply two solid coats of pale terracotta flat latex paint. Use a paintbrush to stipple the edges and niches to imitate the texture offered by a thick pile roller. Lightly sand between coats with wet-and-dry sandpaper.

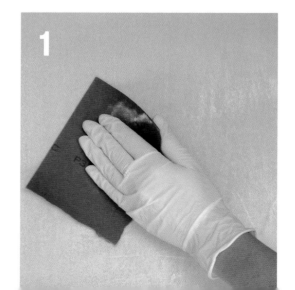

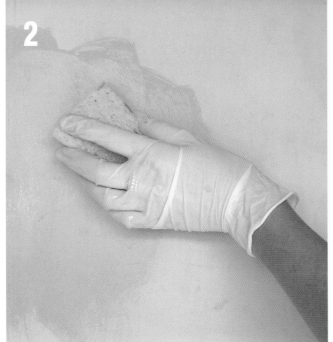

2 APPLYING THE BASE COLOR
Dilute some burnt sienna pigment with water and mix with the matte glaze. The glaze acts as a binder and makes the paint appear slightly transparent. Using a decorators' sponge, apply the first layer of color with a fairly dilute mix over the whole surface. Keep working in the color until dry. Begin sponging on an area that's no larger than 2 x 2 ft. Start the next patch working the glaze up to meet the last patch with a slightly feathered edge to prevent a noticeable line. Use a small brush to work the paint into the edges and corners. Let dry.

3 PAINTING
Add at least one more coat over the whole surface using the same method. When dry, apply a deeper mix of pigment and glaze to the recessed areas and patches here and there to give the walls more depth and variety.

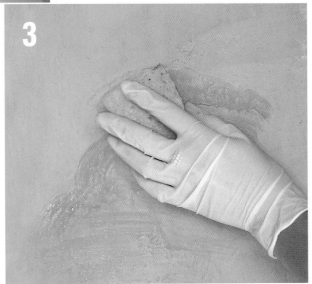

4 Before the paint has dried completely, use a brush to dribble water down the walls to create some random streaking and runs of paintwork. This will lift off some of the color exposing the thinner first layers. Before it is completely dry, gently wipe with a damp sponge and soften the stronger streaks, which may collect in areas. Repeat as necessary until the wall has an unusual random coloration and texture. Let dry.

WEATHERED SIENNA

5 Use a darker mix of pigment and glaze to brush in areas of deeper color here and there, particularly in the niches and at the edges of the walls where color might have naturally avoided wear and tear over the years. Feather the edges of each darker patch with the damp sponge. Repeat as necessary. Let dry.

6 Lightly sand back some areas with wet-and-dry sandpaper to bring back the light base color. This will add to the contrast of tones.

7 Mix some of the base color and glaze in a 1:2 ratio and carefully paint the whole surface with the mix to blend or soften the effect slightly. The glaze should be transparent enough not to sit on the surface. If it forms a milky top coat as it dries, it is too thick and must be diluted with some water. It is best to do a small test area somewhere discreet, first. Let dry.

8 FINISHING
Dilute a low-luster oil varnish with liquid solvent in a 1:2 ratio and apply two coats over the whole surface. Let dry overnight between the layers.

Secondary colors

Try some alternative finishes, such as cross-hatching, fine polished plaster work, or stippling, to bring variety and movement to the secondary colors.

◀ LILAC WASH

While this variation is similar to the technique used in the turquoise verdigris scheme (page 68), the colors used are exactly the same as in the lilac wash scheme (page 32). Apply them with a brush in cross-hatching layers of thin paint.

ORANGE STUCCO PLASTER OVER MARMORINO ▶

Like the red and orange plaster scheme, pale orange colorant is added to lime marmorino plaster and a top coat of fine marble is added. (See page 120.) Apply this stucco lustro plaster when the first two coats of marmorino are nearly dry. Wash yellow and orange colorants repeatedly over the polished plaster with a sponge to vary and intensify the finished look.

◀ STIPPLED GREEN

This effect is created with three colors of green acrylic paint in varying degrees of light and dark. Apply a cream base coat over the surface with a roller. Let dry.

Dip the bristles of a hog hair stippling brush into the dark green paint, and dab off the excess. Stipple the paint on by dabbing the flat of the bristles against the surface. Cover the surface with a light coat, and let dry. Stipple on with the midgreen paint; then continue in graduated layers from deep to light color until the desired effect is achieved. Protect the finish with a matte acrylic glaze.

COLORWASH IN TWO GREENS ▶

Build up thin layers of color in figure-eight movements with a sponge as in the lacquered red glaze scheme. (See page 16.) Let dry between layers. Build up to five layers of alternate light and dark colors; then end with a soft buffed waxed finish.

CHAPTER 3 Combining Color

BALANCE COMPLEMENTARY COLORS, YELLOW AND VIOLET, RED AND GREEN, ORANGE AND BLUE, WITH STYLE.

Conventional decorating advice suggests that you should avoid combining colors that appear opposite each other on the color wheel. These colors, if placed side by side, intensify one another, or if mixed together, subdue or neutralize each other's intensity. However, with some proper planning, the special relationship between these pairs of colors, which always consist of one warm and one cool color of a similar intensity, can result in some wonderful and unusual effects.

In the first scheme, yellow is used as an accent to brighten and enhance the violet interior. The second technique brings two equally intense colors together to great effect by allowing a small amount of red to show through the predominant green. In the last scheme, warm orange and cool blue complement each other beautifully, and some very different textures and surfaces are also combined.

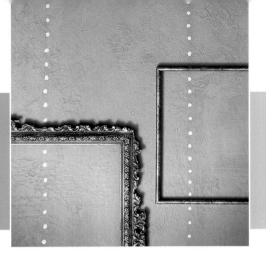

A wall painted with bands of violet may seem too strong a statement for the home. However, adding small highlights of yellow immediately enlivens the violet and brings light and intensity to this exciting effect.

Violet washes with yellow accents

This combination of complementary colors can be extremely successful. Applying violet in thin washes allows the light to reflect off the base color, giving more luminosity. The bands of violet are varied with alternate tints of slightly warmer and cooler colors. A vibrancy is brought to the effect with the addition of the yellow dots. The decorative gold picture frames introduce further accents of yellow, and the metallic and shiny pearlized colors with which they are painted help to sustain the drama. Hallways often lack natural light; the reflective quality of the paint will bounce light off the walls.

Experiment with different washes of color on a sample board with the same base color. Hold the board up against the wall to see the effect of light on the color, and then darken it as necessary.

YOU WILL NEED

For preparation
- Pale, warm blue flat latex paint
- Roller and tray
- Plumb line
- Chalk line
- Straight edge or ruler
- Pencil

For painting
- Warm violet and cool violet flat latex paint
- Medium yellow flat latex paint
- Matte glaze
- Protective gloves
- Decorators' paintbrushes
- Cellulose decorators' sponge
- Paint buckets

MOOD BOARD

Stripes painted experimentally on boards and paper helped produce this mix of colors. The yellow dots of the final decoration were inspired by the effect created when yellow flower petals were dropped against the stripes.

1 PREPARING THE SURFACE

Apply two coats of pale, warm blue flat latex paint over an old plaster wall with a slightly rough texture (this paint effect will also work well on smooth walls). Let dry. Decide where you wish to decorate and drop a plumb line to assess if the walls are level, then create the first straight vertical line. Attach a chalk line to a pin in the wall at the ceiling line and drop it to run parallel with the plumb line. Snap the chalk line to give you a guide to follow for the bands of color. Repeat this in the center of each wall.

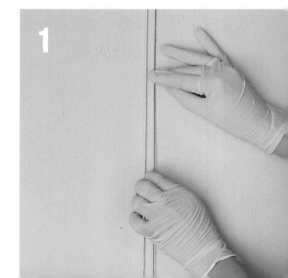

2 MARKING THE WALLS

To create equal, uniform bands of color, measure from the first vertical line using a ruler and pencil, and mark the wall to match up with the next chalk line drop. Repeat around the room.

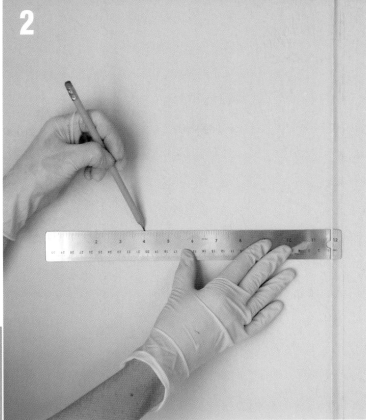

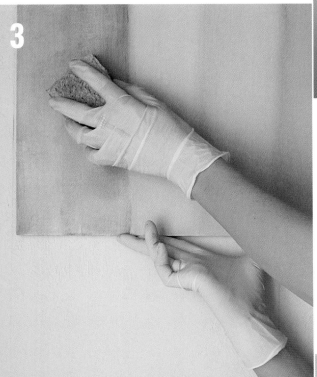

3 PAINTING

Mix the colors by adding some water to each. Experiment first with the colors on a sample board. If using flat latex paint straight from the can, add water in a 1:1 ratio. If working with stronger colors, such as acrylic tubes of paint, it may be necessary to add water in a 1:2 ratio. The aim is to achieve a mix of different violet colors of a similar tone in alternate vertical bands or stripes around the walls. It is better to work with colors that vary in hue while remaining close in tone.

4

Begin to add the first washes of color by applying the paint with a sponge and brush and washing up to the chalk line as neatly as possible. It is best to keep the sponge damp and dilute the colors with a little water to make it easier to work with over large areas.

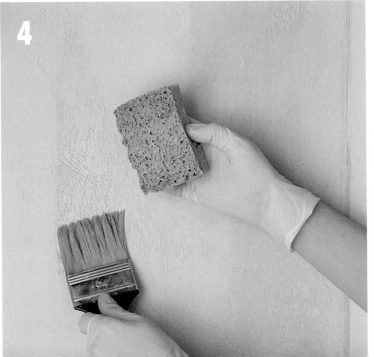

5

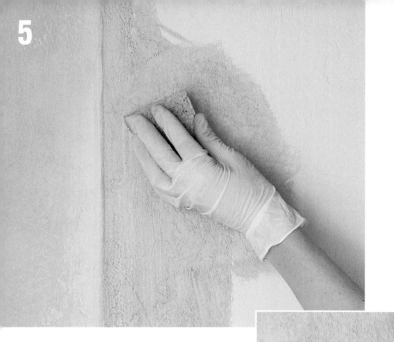

When the first color is completely dry, begin to add deeper colors over the lighter colors. The paint will be easier to apply as the layers are built up. Keep the paints diluted by adding small amounts of water. Apply the paint with a brush, working up to the chalk line each time, then soften the area with the damp sponge. Try to work each band individually from floor to ceiling. Work quickly and evenly to avoid join marks before the paint has dried. You may prefer to work with a partner.

6

When dry, begin to add a final unifying layer of dilute deep violet color over the whole wall. This must be applied with a brush and damp sponge. The paint mix must be very dilute: 1:3 with water. Try not to overload the brush, and work quickly but consistently applying and wiping off the color.

7

Before the paint is completely dry, clean and dampen the sponge. Wipe the paint back smoothly to leave a thin layer.

8

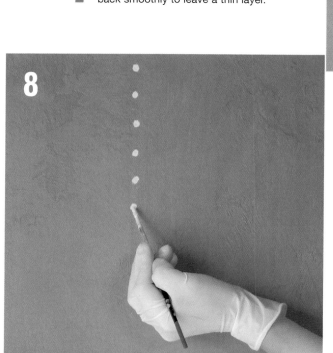

FINISHING

Mix a medium yellow. Using a large or small brush, depending on the size of dot you wish to add, paint a line of dots down the join of the violet and purple bands. Keep the spacing even. This will help disguise any uneven edges and also add an unusual regular highlighting line. Stand back regularly to check if it is straight. Wipe off mistakes quickly with a damp sponge, washing the sponge out regularly. Let dry. Glaze the walls with a matte glaze for extra protection.

A subtle crackle-glaze completes the effect produced by painting a green latex paint over a red base color. The woodwork, painted in red over green, complements the walls. Consider this scheme in a hallway or an area leading to a garden or sunroom.

Crackled poppy red and spring green

Nature can offer some interesting and radical color combinations. Flashes of poppy red against spring green make a vibrant and energetic mix. Find an image that inspires you and add color swatches and a variety of textural finishes to create the mix you wish to achieve in your scheme. Mix a range of different green and red acrylic paints and try out on sample boards or paper. Hold against walls to help you to make design decisions.

Applying a crackle-glaze medium causes the top coat to split in a random pattern to expose the base color. This technique helps to unify the unusual color combination of red and green. The green also makes a wonderful background for dark and warm wood colors and furniture.

YOU WILL NEED

For preparation
- Acrylic primer
- Medium-grade wet-and-dry sandpaper
- Damp cloth
- Decorators' paintbrush

For base color and crackleglaze
- Red flat latex paint
- Green flat latex paint
- Crackle-glaze medium

For painting
- Green flat latex paint
- Yellow acrylic paint
- Matte glaze
- Low-luster oil varnish
- Protective gloves
- Decorators' paintbrushes
- Roller (optional)
- Paint buckets
- Cellulose decorators' sponge
- Hair dryer
- Medium- and fine-grade wet-and-dry sandpaper
- Soft bristle brush
- Lint-free cloth or tack cloth

MOOD BOARD
The beautiful combination of poppy red and textured green suggests the appearance of summer-flowering poppies against the lush green of fields. This effect is inspired by the peeling paint on old fishing boats and driftwood found on beaches.

1 PREPARING THE SURFACE
Wipe down the wall and woodwork with a damp cloth to remove any grease. Using a paintbrush, apply two coats of acrylic primer to the wall and woodwork. Let dry. Lightly sand to a smooth finish. Wipe with a tack cloth.

2 APPLYING THE BASE COLOR
Apply at least two coats of red latex paint on the wall areas using a paintbrush or roller. Apply the paint in regular short strokes in all directions to achieve an even finish. Let dry. Using a paintbrush, apply the green base color to all of the woodwork. Try to achieve an even coverage. Let dry.

3 APPLYING THE CRACKLE-GLAZE
Using a fine paintbrush, apply the crackle-glaze medium over all of the paint. This will dry quickly and must be applied in a good solid layer over the whole surface. Let dry. Apply another thin layer, where needed, if the first coat has not covered completely.

4 PAINTING
When the crackle-glaze medium is dry, apply the green latex paint over all the areas that are painted red. The wet paint will activate the crackle-glaze medium at once so the application of the topcoat needs to be swift. Use quick short brush strokes. Do not return to any area and re-paint it because it will lift the paint and move the crackle-glaze into a wavy lumpy surface. Let settle for a few minutes.

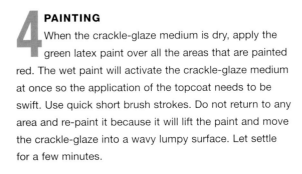

CRACKLED RED AND GREEN

5 Once settled, assist the crackle effect by gently warming the surface with a hair dryer.

6 Apply the red latex paint over the green base color in the same quick, short brush strokes. Try not to brush over the areas that already have a top coat on. Let settle, and then assist the crackle effect with a hair dryer as in Step 5. Let dry overnight.

7 FINISHING
Use medium-grade wet-and-dry sandpaper and then fine-grade to lightly sand over the whole surface to remove any dust and rough particles of the crackle-glaze medium and paint. When the surface is smooth to the touch, wipe with a soft bristle brush.

Make a glaze mix of green latex paint and a touch of yellow acrylic paint mixed with matte glaze in a 2:1 ratio. The green should be slightly brighter. Using a paintbrush and sponge, wash the glaze over the deeper green color. The deep green color will have variations of color because the red base color is showing. The brighter green glaze will lift the colors and give more depth. Lightly sand again and then finally seal with two coats of low-luster oil varnish.

COMBINING COLOR

A simple plastered fireplace is transformed into an interesting focal point by the addition of the blue opalescent tile border, which emphasizes the fireplace opening.

Orange plaster and blue faux tiles

The paint effect used for the soft-orange sienna matte walls and box shape fireplace becomes more obvious in half light and with low lighting, while in bright daylight the effect is more subtle. The movement and texture of the colorwash alters the surface appearance dramatically according to the light.

This technique was devised to suggest the natural color and texture of plaster, or stucco colored with the natural earth pigments of clay. It is a combination often seen in countries such as Morocco and India where buildings are often decorated with clay-based pigments. It brings together a vibrant mix of warm and cool colors, offering a relaxing and harmonious atmosphere.

MOOD BOARD

The intense contrast of warm and cool colors is revealed by some patterned blue tile work against a sienna colorwash. A simple square decoration reduces the work entailed in the effect.

YOU WILL NEED

For preparation
- Pale orange/terracotta flat latex paint
- All-purpose filler or textured masonry paint
- Medium-grade wet-and-dry sandpaper
- Roller and tray

For painting
- Burnt sienna acrylic paint
- Yellow ocher acrylic paint
- Matte acrylic glaze
- Protective gloves
- Decorators' paintbrushes
- Cellulose decorators' sponge
- Paint buckets

For the blue tile decoration
- Pale blue flat latex paint
- Opalescent paint in blue and orange tints
- Cobalt blue acrylic paint
- Burnt umber acrylic paint
- Stencil paper
- Pencil
- Steel ruler and right angle
- Craft knife
- Mat board
- Painters' tape
- Lint-free cloth or tack cloth
- All-purpose filler
- Small artists' brush

1

1 PREPARING THE SURFACE

Mix the base coat, thicken some normal flat latex paint by adding all-purpose filler or use textured masonry paint mixed in a light terracotta color. Apply the paint over the whole surface with a roller. The paint will need at least two coats and a light sanding between coats. Let dry. The surface should be slightly uneven and the topcoat will have a peaked texture. Use a brush and some paint to stipple all the corners and edges.

2

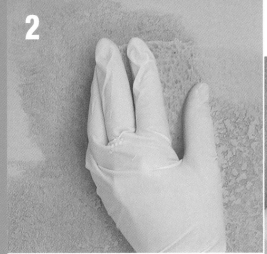

2 PAINTING

Dilute some burnt sienna acrylic paint with water in a 1:2 ratio and begin to apply it in a light wash with a damp sponge. Use a small brush for the corners and edges. Work quickly in circular cloud shapes in a 2 x 2 ft area. The edges should be softened; flip the sponge and wipe again to thin the paint where the next areas will begin. The paint will appear deeper in color where it sits in the holes of the textured base color. Let dry.

3

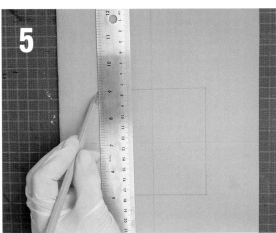

3

Mix some yellow ocher acrylic paint with water in a 1:2 ratio and apply as the first coat of colorwash. Let dry. When the two colors are completely dry check for depth of color and add areas of either color again here and there, particularly if some of the base coat is still showing. When completely dry, sand lightly. This will smooth the surface and expose the base color where any peaks have been knocked off.

4 FINISHING

The paint effect will need glazing to protect it and to reduce any brightness. Dilute the base color with water in a 1:2 ratio and add 1:2 acrylic glaze and mix well. Wash this lightly over the whole surface with a damp sponge. Use a small brush for the corners. Let dry.

4

5

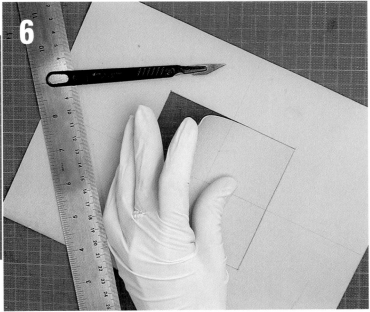

5 APPLYING THE BLUE TILE DECORATION

Measure the area where you will add the blue tile decoration and decide the size of the tiles you will paint. Draw the square on stencil paper with a pencil and steel ruler. Use a right angle to check that it is as accurate as possible.

6

6

Use a sharp craft knife to cut out the shape. Always cut the corners first to avoid any overcutting. Use a mat board and a steel ruler to guide the knife.

7 Measure and mask the border to be decorated with the blue faux tiles. Paint the border with a pale blue flat latex paint thickened slightly with all-purpose filler to give a more solid, smooth surface for the faux tiles. Let dry.

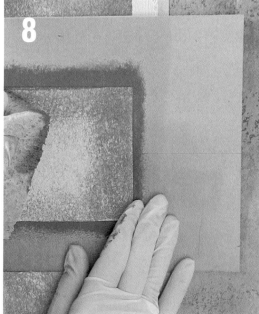

8 Use cobalt blue acrylic paint and a damp sponge to apply thin layers of blue through the stencil. Each layer should be built up with darker blue toward the edges to enhance the illusion of a three-dimensional tile. Let dry between each layer to check the depth of color achieved.

9 Leave the masking tape in place and paint a layer of opalescent blue acrylic over the whole border. Let dry and apply a second layer of opalescent acrylic paint in orange tint, brushed in the other direction to give complete coverage. Let dry, then carefully remove the masking tape.

10 FINISHING Dilute some burnt umber acrylic paint with a little water. Using a small artists' brush, paint along the edge of the tile border to suggest the three-dimensional qualities of applied tiles sitting above the surface of the plaster effect.

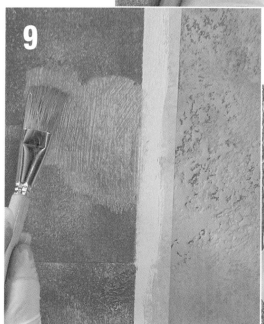

Complementary colors

Explore the intensity that results from combining the complementary colors by working with some interesting techniques.

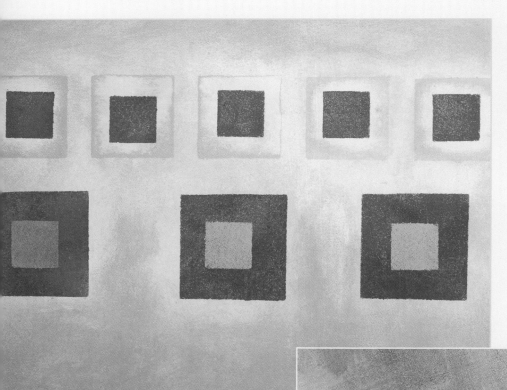

◄ STENCILED SQUARES APPLIED OVER A GREEN COLORWASH

Draw around a stencil onto a piece of cardstock and cut it out with a sharp knife. Always use a mat board and a steel ruler to guide the knife. Using a ruler and pencil, measure and mark out the area where you will add the border design. Use masking tape to fix the stencil to the wall, and lightly apply paint with a sponge.

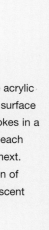

BLUE AND ORANGE ►

Brush blue and pale orange acrylic paint repeatedly across the surface with regular short brush strokes in a cross-hatching pattern. Let each coat dry before adding the next. Finish with a light application of blue and then orange opalescent paint for additional interest.

◄ ORANGE AND PALE BLUE OVER A CREAM BACKGROUND

Using a sponge, apply colorwashed layers of thin paint over a cream background. Dilute pale blue and orange paint with a little water, and apply in alternate layers in figure-eight movements to give a smooth finish. Let dry between layers.

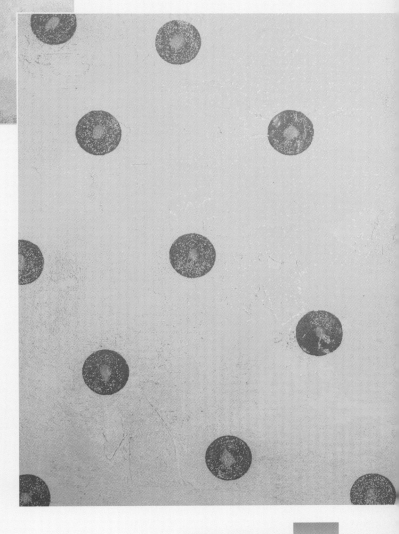

VIOLET SPOTS OVER YELLOW ►

For the background, use a sponge to apply repeated layers of yellow latex paint over the base color until the required density is achieved. Dip the round end of a fine foam radiator roller head into some violet latex paint. Dab off the excess. Lightly press the paint-loaded end onto the surface and remove. Continue to create a random pattern of spots. Let dry. Add a yellow dot in the middle of each violet spot. Sand the pattern lightly to give a smooth finish and seal it with a matte acrylic glaze.

CHAPTER 4 # Mixed and Muted

CREATE TINTS, SHADES, AND TONES TO ENHANCE THE BEAUTY OF
VIBRANT, COMPLEX COLORS.

This chapter introduces the tertiary colors in the color wheel. These

are the more complex colors created by mixing equal parts of primary

and adjacent secondary colors together. For example, red and violet

make crimson, blue and green make turquoise, and yellow and green

make lime. To allow the unusual colors to be appreciated fully, tone

them down gently to fit in with other elements.

 The first scheme creates a faux wood effect on a cupboard by

building up layers of oil glaze and varnish in deep crimson with a

touch of black added. The turquoise verdigris scheme shown next

demonstrates how to soften a bright color by mixing it with white.

The third scheme combines a variety of techniques—washes,

stenciling, and bands of flat color—to create an exuberant lime green

mix with depth and texture.

Give an old cupboard a facelift with a fantasy wood effect decoration by painting it first in a pale pink eggshell finish and then decorating it with a faux wood-grain effect imitating fruitwood.

Crimson faux wood effect

The textures and effects produced in this project recall the characteristic knots and graining of many hardwoods while layers of glaze and varnish give depth and aging. The color used here resembles that of fruitwood but to imitate another wood, simply choose another color.

Most of the texturing is created in the first glaze mix while it is still wet. Once this is dry, repeated layers are built up to achieve the final effect. Different mixes of crimson and black are dragged over the graining and knotting to add more texture. The final two smooth layers of varnish and crimson lift and brighten the darker first coat, adding some zing. Each layer is lightly sanded between coats.

YOU WILL NEED

For preparation
- Pale pink oil-based eggshell paint
- Artists' oil paint: crimson, burnt umber, and black
- Liquid solvent
- Fine-grade wet-and-dry sandpaper
- Fine foam roller and tray

For wood effect
- Low-luster oil varnish
- Heart-graining tool
- Protective gloves
- Decorators' paintbrushes including pointed fitch; hog hair softening brush
- Paint buckets
- Rubber comb
- Fine-grade wet-and-dry sandpaper
- Lint-free soft cloth or tack cloth

MOOD BOARD

Wooden items and samples of colored wood stains decided the color and patterning of the fruitwood effect. Every wood has its own unique character of knots and graining, so mix and match elements to create your own effect.

1 PREPARING THE SURFACE

Apply the pale pink eggshell paint with a fine foam roller. The paint will need at least two coats. Let dry between coats and lightly sand the surface. To make the red-brown wood color, mix together some crimson, burnt umber, and black oil paints, and then make a glaze mix of the red-brown paint and liquid solvent in a 1:2 ratio. Using a paintbrush, apply the glaze over the first panel and then drag the paintbrush back through the wet glaze to make straight lines in one direction.

2 CREATING THE WOOD EFFECT

Hold the paintbrush at a right angle to the surface of the panel and push the bristles into the glaze so they splay out, creating texture and a random irregular graining effect. Repeat this over the surface at regular intervals, pulling the brush in one direction, occasionally, to create a repeated vertical movement.

3

The next step must take the previous shapes into account. Use a heart-graining tool to create the knots and more obvious wood graining. Pull the tool through the glaze, pivoting the head as you drag it down vertically. Vary the pressure and pivot the head at different angles to avoid a regular pattern. Try to emphasize the waves and vertical graining lines created in the first two steps.

4

Wrap a lint-free cloth over a finger and press it into the glaze to create the "eye" of each knot. Twist the finger slightly to lightly remove the glaze.

CRIMSON FAUX WOOD EFFECT

5 Use a paintbrush to lightly drag some glaze crosswise into the vertical graining. This will add some character to the surface and will also slightly break up any over-dramatic heart graining.

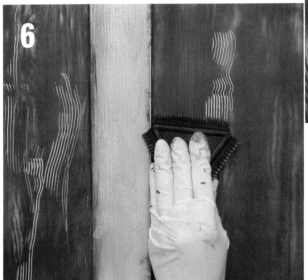

6 With a rubber comb, pull through the heart graining and break up the darker areas of collected glaze to produce a more uniform overall appearance.

7 Use a small fitch paintbrush to add dark patches in the eyes and to exaggerate the knots.

8 FINISHING
Use either a badger hair or hog hair softening brush to lightly soften the texture. Go over the whole surface in different directions. Let dry. Once dry, mix some crimson paint and low-luster oil varnish together in a 1:3 ratio and dilute with a little liquid solvent. Apply at least two coats to protect the surface and enhance the red color. Let dry and lightly sand between coats.

Turquoise is such an unusual, bright color that it will dominate any scheme. Its impact can be softened either by keeping it on a small scale and balancing it with other elements or by adding texture and tinting it with white.

Turquoise verdigris

This project demonstrates two different techniques. The verdigris effect is a simple process of brushing on a special copper patinating fluid of copper sulfate, which will react to give the copper paint a blue-white powdery finish. To protect the patina, carefully seal with a low-luster oil varnish. The main wall effect is another form of painted faux metal patina. This can easily be lightened or darkened at any stage according to requirement. The back of the shelf unit is painted in a turquoise flat latex paint, which is balanced by the surrounding white and thin copper line. All the colors vary in scale and texture and the overall appearance is quite complex. But because no particular element dominates, the effect is easy on the eye.

YOU WILL NEED

For preparation
- Pale blue flat latex paint
- Foam roller and tray
- Medium-grade wet-and-dry sandpaper
- Paintbrush

For patina
- Red oxide primer
- Copper metallic paint
- Turquoise flat latex paint
- White latex paint for mixing
- Copper patination fluid
- Water-based glaze
- Low-luster oil varnish
- Protective gloves, goggles and face mask
- Decorators' paintbrushes
- Paint buckets
- Pencil
- Ruler
- Painters' tape
- Lint-free cloth or tack cloth

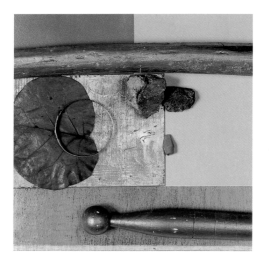

MOOD BOARD

Turquoise is a bright choice for a kitchen. Balancing it with copper metallic colors, patinas, and dark slate flooring subtly alters the effect from slightly frivolous to a refined, clean, and utilitarian workspace.

1 PREPARING THE SURFACE
Apply the pale blue flat latex paint with a roller and paintbrush. The paint will need at least two coats. Let dry and lightly sand between coats to achieve a smooth finish. Let dry.

2 MEASURING THE COPPER BAND

Measure where you wish the top of the copper band to be and mark the wall with a horizontal line. Mask above the line with tape.

3 PREPARING THE BASE COLOR

Brush on a coat of red oxide primer as a base color for the copper paint. This will give the copper a rich dark background and enhance the copper shine. It will dry quickly.

4 APPLYING THE COPPER PAINT

Using a paintbrush, apply two coats of copper metallic paint over the top of the red oxide. Brush in a cross-hatch pattern to achieve the best coverage and for an even overall look. Let dry.

5

Remove the original tape and protect the paint by taping again below the line. Mark and tape another band about 4 in. below the line. This marks out the copper band, which acts as a border between the patinas.

6 Begin to apply the first coat of turquoise flat latex paint in an irregular cross-hatching pattern with threads of color horizontally and vertically above the copper paint. Always use the darkest color first and apply in patches over the whole area. Let dry.

7 Once dry, add the next coat of turquoise, which has been mixed with some white latex paint in a 2:1 ratio. Apply as the previous layer with an irregular cross-hatching pattern. Let dry.

8 Apply the copper paint sparingly in the same way here and there over the top of the turquoise. Keep the brush strokes short and as straight as possible. Use the paintbrush lightly and do not apply too much paint each time to avoid covering up too much of the first color. Let dry.

9 Apply the top coat mixture of turquoise and white paint. Apply as the previous layers but keep the brush strokes even lighter. The paint should sit over the previous layers as a softening layer. Let dry, then protect with two coats of water-based glaze.

10 FINISHING
Add the copper patination fluid over the copper paint below the painted patination. Begin below the second line of tape and brush down in short strokes. Always wear protective gloves, goggles, and a face mask when using any chemicals. When the first wash of fluid has begun to dry, add another coat of fluid. Try to keep your brush strokes as straight and vertical as possible as the patina will follow the runs of the fluid down the wall. Let dry overnight and then seal with a low-luster oil varnish.

In this scheme, the walls are painted in a vibrant lime green mix. Yellow and green tints are then washed over the top. The layers of color are easily and creatively built up and give the effect depth and texture.

Lime green washes

This lime green effect is reached by building up combinations of layered colors in an uncalculated way. As one colorwash changes the character of the previous layer, other elements are adapted and softened with another tinted color. The final product shows the texture and variety of all the reworking. It is a great opportunity to play with different tones and shades of green; you will find it is difficult to decide on a final color. The choices are endless!

If you are short of time, prepare some boards or heavy duty lining paper with the same pale green base color and try out different colorwashes on these first. Hold the samples up against the wall at different times of day and with alternative light sources to make your final decision. Otherwise, enjoy developing subtle differences with small additions of white or yellow to the original color. Use the wall as your mixing board.

YOU WILL NEED

For preparation
- Pale green flat latex paint
- Roller and tray
- Fine-grade wet-and-dry sandpaper
- Lime green and pale green flat oil-based paint
- Cadmium yellow glaze mix

For painting
- Lime green flat latex paint
- Matte acrylic glaze
- Protective gloves
- Decorators' paintbrushes
- Cellulose decorators' sponge
- Paint buckets

For the stencil
- Graph paper
- Stencil paper or acetate
- Pencil
- Measuring tape
- Steel ruler
- Painters' tape
- Stencil brush
- Craft knife
- Mat board

MOOD BOARD

The huge range of lime and pale green-yellows can make a specific choice difficult. Here, the faded leaves inspired the use of a combination of washes rather than just one color.

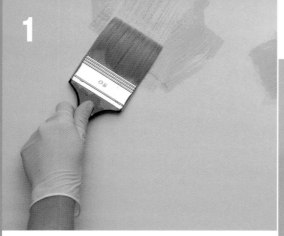

1 PREPARING THE SURFACE
Using a roller, apply at least two coats of pale green flat latex paint to the walls. Lightly sand with fine-grade wet-and-dry sandpaper. Paint the baseboard and windows in lime green and pale green flat oil-based paint. Make a mix of cadmium yellow acrylic and water in a 2:1 ratio. Using a paintbrush, apply paint in random patches, brushing it on and quickly softening it with a sponge while wet. Let dry.

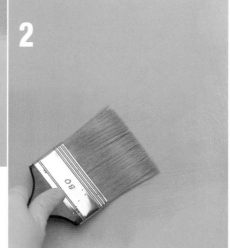

2 APPLYING THE LIME GREEN COLORWASH
Mix the lime green flat latex paint with acrylic glaze in a 2:1 ratio to give a slightly transparent color. Dilute the mix with water, again in a 2:1 ratio, and apply over the walls in the same way as before. Patches of lime green should overlap with the yellow first coat. Finally, soften with a sponge. Let dry.

3 APPLYING THE GLAZE
Make a glaze mix of the lime green glaze and the diluted yellow in a 1:1 ratio. Using a paintbrush, wash over the walls in a smooth regular motion, then soften with a sponge. Use a small brush to apply the glaze mix to the edges and then soften with the sponge. Let dry.

4 Repeat any of the previous steps as required until you reach the desired depth of color and texture. The paint can also be rubbed back to the first wash in patches, which will add texture and variation to the overall look. Using a damp sponge, gently rub over areas in a circular motion, rinsing out the sponge in water occasionally.

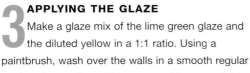

5 STENCILING
Use a pencil and ruler to measure and mark the wall at dado height, then mask with painters' tape above the pencil line. You can also mark and mask a band around the doors or windows in the room if you like.

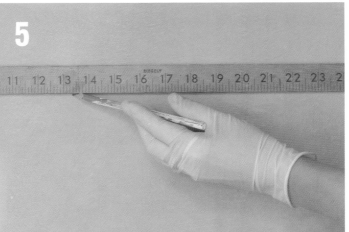

6 Use the lime green paint and a damp sponge to wash one or two layers of a deeper color below the masking tape. Let each layer dry. Keep the layer of colorwash as smooth as possible by using a circular movement and keep rinsing the sponge out in water to avoid it becoming clogged with paint. You can apply the same method to add a deeper green band around the edge of the door and windows trim.

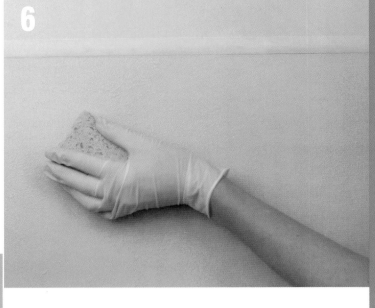

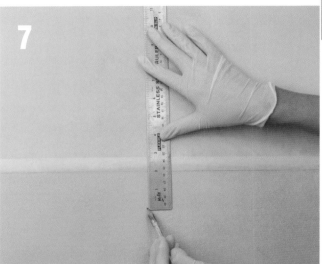

7 Use a pencil and steel ruler to measure and mark another line below the first one. Mask with tape to allow a band for decorating about 2 in. wide.

8 You can use either a ready-made stencil of your choice or you can mark and cut your own, using a sharp knife and stencil paper or acetate. To draw a geometric design, it is easiest to use graph paper, and then trace onto cardboard or photocopy the design onto acetate. Always cut the corners first to avoid any mistakes. Use a mat board and steel ruler to guide the knife.

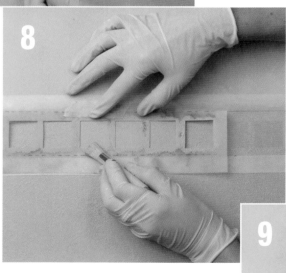

9 FINISHING
Make a color by mixing the lime green with white paint in a 5:1 ratio. Attach the stencil within the band area and use a stenciling brush or small piece of sponge to apply the color. Repeat along the length of the band. Keep repeating with slightly different colors of lime green until you reach the balance of tone you desire.

MIXED AND MUTED

Tertiary colors

Bring depth and sophistication to these unusual colors by creating tints and shades. Some other suggested finishes here include an alternative faux wood effect and subtle layers of colorwash.

◄ MAHOGANY IN CRIMSON AND BROWN

Apply an oil-based eggshell base coat to the surface of some panels in at least two coats. Let dry, and sand after each coat. Mix together alizarin crimson and burnt sienna oil paint for the mahogany red-brown shade; then mix this with liquid solvent in a 1:1 ratio. Brush this glaze onto the first panel.

Mix a darker glaze with crimson and burnt umber; then dilute it with equal parts of liquid solvent. Brush this into the center and the outer edges of the panel. Use a dry brush to scrub into the glaze in successive arcs, repeating the curve to suggest the grain of the real tree where the branch leaves the main trunk.

Use a softening brush to gently blur the lines of the brush strokes. Use a dry brush to drag straight graining effects at the edge of the panel to suggest the straight grain that would be apparent on either side of the arc grain. Soften it off again and let dry. Deepen the effect by adding the darker glaze over the edges and center of the panel and softening in again. Seal it with at least two layers of protective eggshell oil varnish.

TURQUOISE AND WHITE COLORWASH ►

This technique is similar to that used in the lacquered red glaze scheme. (See page 16.) Apply a base coat of pale cream, and leave to dry; then apply a coat of turquoise acrylic paint diluted with a little water to the surface with a sponge.

Mix some turquoise acrylic paint with a touch of white latex paint in a 2:1 ratio to soften the color, and then apply to the surface. Let dry. Add further layers of paint diluted with white alternately with the plain turquoise paint until you achieve the desired effect.

◄ LIME GREEN COLORWASH

Apply repeated layers of green over a pale green base color. Let dry between layers. Apply random repeated lines of yellow/lime paint using a fine fitch brush pulled vertically along a straightedge over the surface.

VERDIGRIS ►

Prepare the surface by applying solid coats of red oxide or red/orange flat latex paint as evenly as possible; then apply a solid coat of copper water-based paint. Let dry.

Use a sponge to dab on an uneven layer of aquamarine blue acrylic paint. Sponge on another uneven layer, this time with a lighter mix of aquamarine blue and white paint. Allow areas of copper to show through. Let dry. Add an equal amount of water to both the copper and aquamarine blue paint, and puddle the paint randomly on the surface by both spattering the paint with a small brush and squeezing out a sponge dipped in each color. Dab off some of the places where it has become too watery.

While the diluted paint is still wet, dust some whiting over the surface. To keep the whiting fine, put a small amount into a strainer and lightly shake this over the wet paint. This will help it adhere to the surface. When the surface is completely dry, protect it with varnish.

VARIATIONS

CHAPTER 5

Natural Color & Texture

EXPERIMENT WITH EARTH AND MINERAL COLORS AND UNUSUAL TECHNIQUES TO CREATE SOME REMARKABLE FAUX FINISHES.

These finishes aim to deceive the eye, using earth and mineral colors to create the illusion of a natural material like stone or rusted iron. Look at examples of the real thing first, and complete some sample boards before beginning. Some of the effects are reached by building up surface texture with thickened paints, but all are still smooth to the touch and easy to live with.

The schemes here range from a fantasy rusted iron finish through some beautifully tactile suede effect panels to a perfect illusion imitating the appearance of the weight and substance of a real stone fire surround.

A simple screen, acting as a room divider between the kitchen and dining room, is given a dramatic faux finish with layers of texture and built up colors to imitate the coloration and other aging effects seen in rusted iron.

Rusted iron effect

This technique can be applied to any surface, but it is shown to the greatest effect on a flat or curved smooth surface. Preparation is important. The surface must be as smooth as possible, with no holes or cracks. A coat of acrylic primer is applied, followed by two coats of red oxide primer which is similar in color to the deeper rust coloration that naturally occurs on old iron. The layers of texture and colors must be thin and smooth to keep the surface even for the protective beeswax sealant. The wax finish softens the contrast of matte and shiny effects produced by the blackboard paint, flat gray undercoat, oxide primer, and the metallic paint. It is a hardwearing surface and can be wiped down with a damp cloth to remove any dust or marks.

The effect can be created in a huge range of colors and tones. Make your decision easier by studying a sample of the real thing, then try to limit your palette of colors to no more than five, or you may never be able to stop re-working the effect!

YOU WILL NEED

For preparation
- Fine filler
- Acrylic primer
- Red oxide metal primer
- Liquid solvent
- Fine-grade wet-and-dry sandpaper

For painting
- Blackboard paint
- Gray undercoat
- Burnt umber acrylic paint
- Acrylic copper paint
- Protective gloves
- Decorators' paintbrushes
- Cellulose decorators' sponge
- Paint buckets
- Real bristle nailbrush
- Beeswax
- Lint-free soft cloth or tack cloth

MOOD BOARD

The coloring for the curved screen was inspired by combining all the decorative elements of the room. The floor tiles and ethnic objects suggest hints of color that will enhance the whole scheme.

1 PREPARING THE SURFACE

Fill any cracks or holes with filler, and once dry, sand lightly for as smooth a surface as possible. Apply a coat of acrylic primer and let dry. Add a little liquid solvent to the red oxide primer to slightly dilute it, then wash this over the surface with a paintbrush, brushing in all directions to achieve an even coverage. Let dry.

2 Repeat the first step with another thin layer of red oxide. Run your hand over the first coat to make sure it is smooth to the touch. If there are any dust particles, lightly sand with very fine wet-and-dry sandpaper and wipe clean before applying the second coat. Let dry.

3 PAINTING

Pour a little blackboard paint into a shallow container. Dip a slightly damp sponge into the paint, then lightly dab the surface here and there. Soften the dabbed paint by lightly rubbing the edges of each patch. These should be the appearance of dark clouds. Let dry.

4 Pour some gray undercoat into another shallow container and dip another slightly damp sponge into the paint. Using the same method as Step 3, add areas of gray paint over and around the black cloud shapes. Dab the gray on lightly here and there to offer a stippled appearance over the surface. Leave some areas of red oxide showing. Let dry.

5 Apply a general wash of burnt umber acrylic paint over the whole surface using another damp sponge. This will adhere to the various paint surfaces in lighter and darker patches. Repeat if required. Let dry.

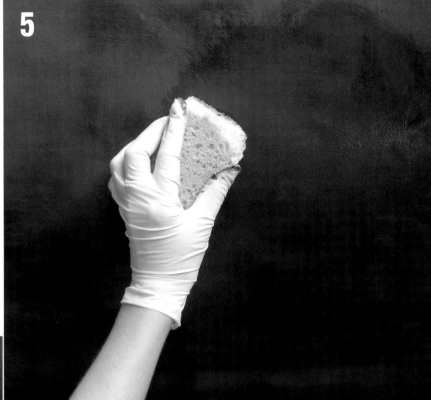

6 Apply a little red oxide to another damp sponge and lightly stipple as a highlight. Try to produce a random dappled effect to create more shapes in the general texture of the surface. Let dry.

7 FINISHING
Pour some of the acrylic copper paint into a shallow container, then dip a hair bristle nailbrush into the paint. Do not overload the brush. Lightly run your fingers along the bristles to spray a fine spatter of paint over the surface. Give most of the surface a light spattering while covering some areas more densely. Let dry overnight, then protect the surface from damage with a thin layer of beeswax applied with a soft cloth and buffed with another clean soft cloth.

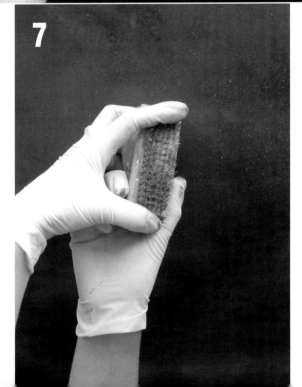

This is a simple method to add texture to a large area with the least amount of effort. The suede effect adds depth to the colorwashes and creates an interesting and unusual finish without dominating the room.

Suede effect panels

Here, the different textures are achieved with rollers. The textured paint may be washed over with any variety of colors to imitate stone, leather, suede, or textured fabric. Run your hand over the surface of the finished effect to experience the smooth, tactile feeling of the sanded surface. To achieve the required depth of texture and color, it is best to experiment with colorwashes and sanding on sample boards first. Examine samples of the surface you wish to imitate under different light sources.

Decide on the size of panels you wish to work with and measure the area carefully to ensure they are in proportion to doorways, windows, baseboard, and furniture. Unify the final effect with repeated washes of thin glaze over the whole surface. Very thin layers are best because they are easier to control.

MOOD BOARD

A paneled or checkered pattern has already been imagined on the walls. The aim is to create something smooth to the touch, both unusual and sensual. Collections of fabric and leather samples suggest different textures.

YOU WILL NEED

For preparation
- Beige flat latex paint
- Dark taupe flat latex paint
- Paint-texturing additive
- Sheepskin and foam rollers and trays

For the texture
- Light taupe flat latex paint
- Rubber texturing pad
- Burnt umber acrylic paint
- Matte acrylic glaze
- Protective gloves
- Decorators' paintbrushes
- Cellulose decorators' sponge
- Paint buckets
- Fine-grade wet-and-dry sandpaper

For measuring
- Pencil
- Measuring tape
- Steel ruler
- Craft knife
- Painters' tape

1 PREPARING THE SURFACE

Apply two coats of beige flat latex paint with a foam roller. Mix the paint-texturing additive with the dark taupe flat paint, a little at a time to avoid lumps. The thickness of the texture is up to you—a creamy consistency works well. Mix enough for a day's work because the mix will dry out overnight. Pour the mix into a roller tray and roll on with the sheepskin roller to give the first coat a heavy texture.

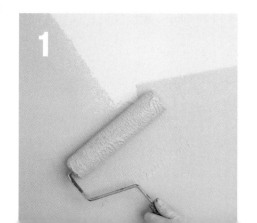

2 APPLYING THE TEXTURE

To keep the texture even over the whole surface to be decorated, use a small brush to stipple the paint into corners and edges. Gently work the wet paint with a rubber texturing pad so the surface is consistently marked with peaked thick paint. Let dry.

3 If it becomes apparent that the paint is too thin in areas, re-apply the thickened paint where it is required once the first coat is dry.

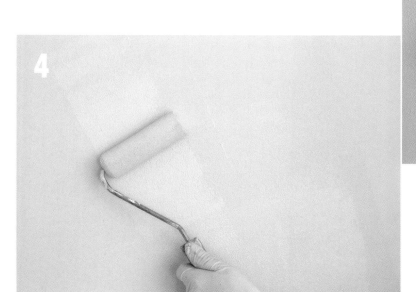

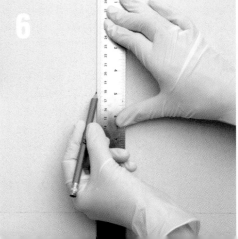

4 When the first coat is completely dry, apply the lighter taupe color with a fine foam roller. Let dry and repeat where patches of the first coat show through. Let dry.

6 MEASURING THE PANELS

Use a steel ruler and pencil to measure and carefully mark the square panels. The effect is best if each square is at least 16 in. in size but it is more important that the squares fit the area neatly and are in proportion to other features in the room.

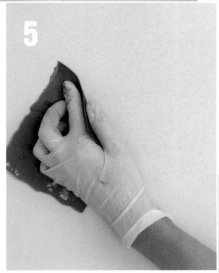

5 Lightly sand the whole wall with fine-grade wet-and-dry sandpaper. This will knock off the peaks of the first textured paint layer and expose the deeper color underneath, creating extra depth and texture.

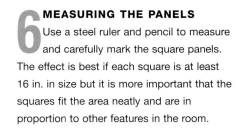

7 Use painters' tape to protect the edge of each alternate panel. The tape may not adhere well to the textured surface, so check the adhesion before painting. Cut the tape carefully at each corner to make a straight, sharp line.

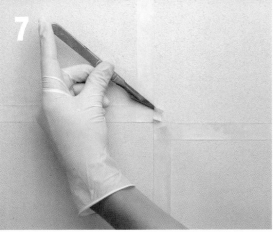

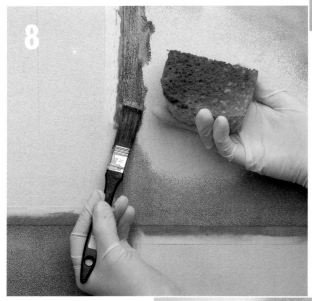

8 Mix some burnt umber paint with acrylic glaze in a 1:2 ratio and use a sponge to apply it to each untaped panel. Use a paintbrush to form a darker edge near the tape, feathering out into the center of each panel with the sponge. Let dry.

9 Remove the tape from the first panels, then mask the rest. Repeat the process until all the panels have been washed with the colored glaze.

10 Remove the tape from the whole wall carefully, checking the line near the tape to see if the color has taken neatly.

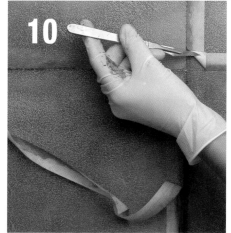

11 FINISHING Use fine-grade wet-and-dry sandpaper to gently sand the whole area again. The lighter second coat will show through the darker glazed layer. Finally, glaze the whole area once more with the burnt umber and glaze mix.

NATURAL COLOR & TEXTURE

An old fireplace is transformed into a stunning focal point by the addition of an imitation stone surround suggesting the permanence and solidity of real stone, but at only a fraction of the cost.

Stone effect fire surround

This technique can be used to great effect on any well-prepared surface and offers flexibility and variety. The coloration can be as strong or subtle as required. Simply add washes of color and spattering until the required effect is achieved. The paint is protected with two coats of low-luster oil varnish, which will darken the final color slightly.

The textured paint mix must be made up in batches on the day it's used because it will quickly dry out. Always scrape out any excess and dispose of it in the garbage. Never wash it down the sink.

YOU WILL NEED

For preparation
- Acrylic primer
- Fine-grade wet-and-dry sandpaper

For textured paint
- Pale beige flat latex paint
- Paint-texturing additive
- Straight-edged cardboard

For painting
- Burnt umber acrylic paint
- Bronze metallic acrylic paint
- White flat latex paint
- Low-luster oil varnish
- Protective gloves
- Decorators' paintbrushes
- Paint buckets
- Cellulose decorators' sponge
- Fine-grade wet-and-dry sandpaper
- Real bristle nailbrush
- Soft bristle brush

MOOD BOARD
Examine some natural stone to see the color variations that provide its unique character. The simple pale wood effect floor tiles enhance the warmth of the fireplace surround.

1 PREPARING THE SURFACE

Apply two coats of acrylic primer to the surface, letting it dry and sanding lightly between coats. Make a mix of the beige base color and the textured paint additive. This should be added slowly and mixed in well to avoid lumps. Only mix enough to cover the area that is to be decorated because the mix will dry out overnight.

2 APPLYING THE TEXTURED PAINT

Use a paintbrush and sponge to stipple the mixture over the whole surface. Work carefully and consistently to try to achieve an even finish. Let dry.

3

Repeat the texturing over the whole surface quite thickly. Before the mix has dried completely, use a strip of straight-edged cardboard to gently pull through the texture, flattening some areas by knocking off the stippled peaks. Let dry.

4 PAINTING

Dilute the burnt umber paint with water in a 1:3 ratio. Use a paintbrush and sponge to wash on and wipe away the color, leaving a buildup of color in the recesses. Let dry. Dilute the bronze metallic acrylic paint in the same ratio and apply in the same way. Let dry.

STONE EFFECT FIRE SURROUND

5

5 When completely dry, lightly sand the surface with fine-grade wet-and-dry sandpaper to expose the beige base color as a regular mottled texture.

6 SPATTERING
Pour some of the burnt umber paint into a shallow container and dip the nailbrush into the paint. With your finger, pull back the bristles lightly and spatter the color over the surface, to suggest the variety of color seen in stone.

7

6

7 Repeat this technique with the beige base color and a touch of white. Let dry overnight.

8 FINISHING
Lightly sand again, then dust with a soft bristle brush. Apply at least two coats of low-luster oil varnish for protection.

8

NATURAL COLOR & TEXTURE

Natural colors

By reminding us of the natural environment, earth and mineral tones and textures have a soothing effect in the home. Try a range of techniques to realize their potential.

◄ STONE BLOCK EFFECT

As in the suede effect scheme on page 84, apply the base color; then measure and mark out the appropriate size stone block work. Tape over the lines with fine graph tape, and cut the tape neatly with a craft knife where it overlaps into the block work.

Mix some paint with enough paint texturing additive to reach a creamy consistency. Pour it into a roller tray, and use a sheepskin roller to apply the paint to the whole surface, including over the tape. Let dry.

Remove the tape gently, aiming to keep the lines crisp. This will show the base color as the grouting line. Lightly sand over the whole surface with wet-and-dry sandpaper to knock off the peaks of the textured paint. Wipe over the surface with a damp sponge; then seal it with matte varnish.

METAL PATINA ►

Apply a gray undercoat, and then, using a sponge, wash some patches of burnt umber acrylic paint and copper acrylic paint over the surface. Ensure that areas of the gray undercoat are still visible.

Dab on patches of silver paint with a sponge, and smooth in here and there, overlapping the other colors to produce a shimmer.

Spatter the surface with copper and the burnt umber acrylic paint to suggest age spots. Dust some whiting through a strainer over the surface of the wet paint. Let dry and brush off any excess. Protect the finish with varnish.

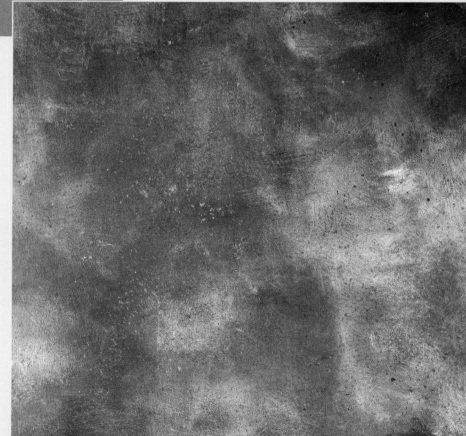

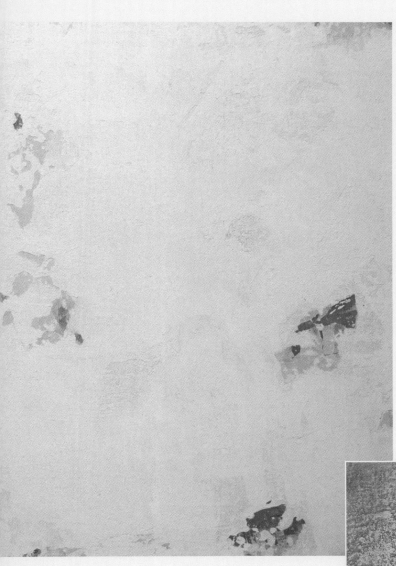

◄ PLASTER EFFECT OVER A TERRACOTTA BASE

Apply a thin coat of terracotta flat latex paint over the surface with a brush or, alternatively, sponge over a pale off-white coat of flat latex paint with a roller. Let dry.

Divide some one-coat plaster mix into two batches. Add a little gray colorant to one batch and a little yellow ocher to the other to give a light cream color. Use a plasterers' hawk and trowel to apply a thin, irregular layer of the gray plaster, allowing the base color to show in random areas. Let dry.

Repeat the process with a top coat of the cream plaster, allowing areas of base color and the gray first coat of plaster to show through. Use a small filling knife to add random patches of cream, gray, and natural plaster color. Keep the applicators clean by regularly wiping with a damp cloth. When it's completely dry, sand lightly with wet-and-dry sandpaper and seal with a transparent matte varnish or acrylic glaze.

STONE EFFECT ►

Create a variation on the stone effect scheme using different colors. (See page 88.) Apply two coats of acrylic primer to the surface. Let dry, and lightly sand between coats.

Mix a cream base color and some textured paint additive, and apply it over the whole surface. Work carefully and consistently to try to achieve an even finish. Let dry.

Dilute burnt sienna paint with water in a 1:3 ratio and some yellow ocher acrylic paint in the same ratio. Use a paintbrush and sponge to wash on and wipe away the color, leaving a buildup of color in the recesses. Let dry.

Add washes of color and spattering until the required effect is achieved. Protect the paint with two coats of low-luster oil-based varnish, which will darken the final color slightly.

CHAPTER 6 Monochromatic Style

A ONE-COLOR SCHEME OFFERS TRANQUILITY IN THE HOME; SOME INTERESTING EFFECTS WILL BRING THE COLOR TO LIFE.

Using just one color leaves you free to experiment with texture, shape, pattern, and scale in your scheme. The use of crackle finishes, distressed paint effects, and shimmering metallic and opalescent paints, together with unusual panels, borders, stripes, and strong graphic lines will add interest and individuality to a limited palette.

Each of these three schemes offers a simple off-white or monochromatic scheme and uses some easily achievable techniques. While the actual surface texturing and paint effects are busy and varied and give much more interest than a flat color when light hits them, the markings are generally not visible from a distance, and the simplicity of the colors results in a finish that is relaxing and serene.

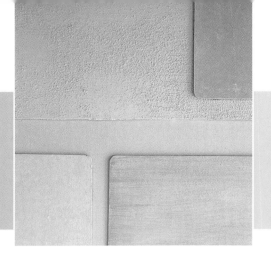

Inspired by the colors of the sea and the reflective effects of light on water, this wall panel will add interest to any room. A variety of geometric shapes in different colors and textures are fixed onto a panel and blue iridescent paint is used as a highlight.

Blue-gray geometric panel

In this project, each cardboard shape has been treated to a different surface texture, color, and finish—silver, iridescent blue, matte blue, multi blue-gray washes, and stippled colors. The monochrome simplicity of the decoration allows more experimentation with matte, shiny, and textured finishes to add interest to the wall panel. Mark out a simple plan of the design and then cut the pieces out of cardboard; cut some extra pieces to allow for experimentation. Each cardboard piece is left free to be repositioned as required until the final step. However, the pieces could just as easily be glued down to the base from the beginning. The canvas stretcher used as a base here was given two coats of color and allowed to dry before adhering the decorated pieces.

The color palette is restricted to three basic blue-gray colors plus silver. The cardboard is primed on both sides to prevent the surface from warping, and the pieces variously textured with stippling, dragging, sponging, and puddling some areas with thick paint. After laying these out as desired, ready to be glued with contact adhesive, some are given a wash of iridescent blue.

YOU WILL NEED

For preparation
- Acrylic primer
- Fine-grade wet-and-dry sandpaper
- Paint roller and tray

For drawing
- Thick, acid-free, gray cardboard
- Pencil
- Steel ruler
- Craft knife
- Mat board

For painting
- Acrylic silver and iridescent blue paint
- Pale blue, gray blue, and pastel blue flat latex paint
- All-purpose filler
- Paint-texturing additive
- Pastel blue thick latex paint
- Contact adhesive
- Protective gloves
- Decorators' paintbrushes
- Cellulose decorators' sponge
- Paint buckets
- Wet-and-dry sandpaper

MOOD BOARD
The soft, worn colors of these muted off-white, tarnished silver, and gray painted samples, photographs, and sun-bleached pebbles are a reminder of winter days spent at the seaside.

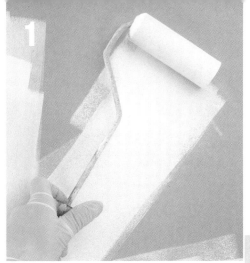

1 PREPARING THE SURFACE

Begin by measuring and deciding on the scale of the panel you wish to create. Use a roller to add a coat of acrylic primer to the board or canvas. Let dry, then lightly sand to a smooth finish. (Optional: Apply two coats of chosen background color.) Select a large enough piece of cardboard from which to cut shapes and apply a coat of acrylic primer to both sides. Let dry.

2 DRAWING THE SHAPES

Draw out the shapes on the cardboard. You can use other shapes to draw around or measure and mark out with a pencil and steel ruler.

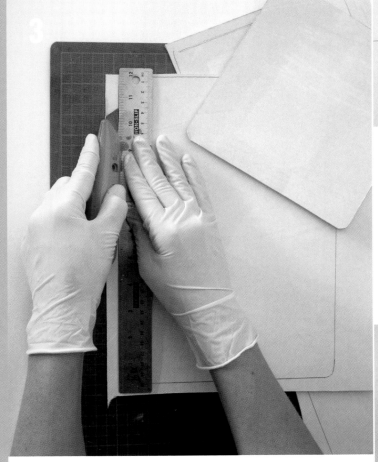

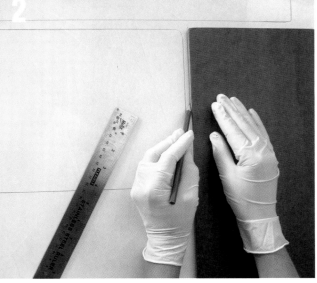

3 CUTTING OUT

Cut out the cardboard shapes with a craft knife. Always cut the corners first to avoid any overcutting. Use a mat board and a steel ruler to guide the knife.

4

Apply a second coat of acrylic primer, including the cut edges, to the shapes. Let dry.

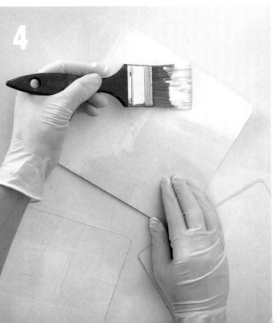

5 PAINTING

Choose the colors you wish to use and try them out together on samples. Paint the pieces of cardboard with the first coat of color and let dry.

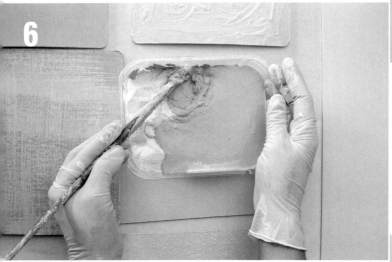

6

Prepare mixes of various textures and colors for the shapes. For some shapes, add all-purpose filler mix to flat latex paint in a 3:1 ratio. Add some paint-texturing additive (see page 11) to flat latex paint to paint some shapes and use pastel blue thick latex paint on other shapes. Let dry.

7

Choose the shapes you wish to paint silver and sand the background color to achieve a smooth surface. Use a brush or sponge to apply the silver paint smoothly. The iridescent blue paint can be washed over a colored background. Let dry.

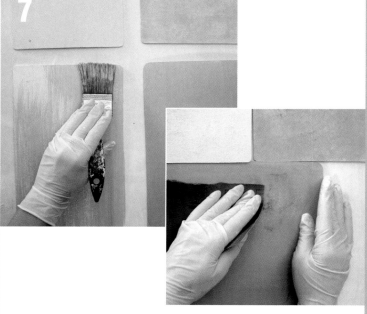

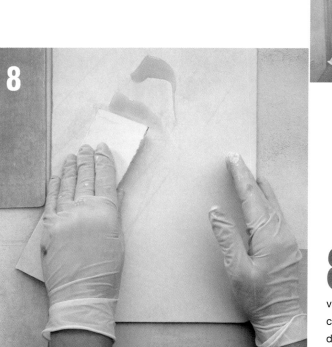

8 FINISHING

Add texture to the surface of some shapes by sanding in different directions and with varied pressure to give pattern and depth to the color and to soften off any shapes that are too dominant or bright. Position and glue the shapes with contact adhesive. Add weights to hold down the cardboard for a firm grip.

MONOCHROMATIC STYLE

Tongue-and-groove paneling on walls and furniture are painted in pale pink, blue, and off-white, and treated with crackle-glaze and aging effects to achieve a look reminiscent of a simple Scandinavian painted interior.

Pink and off-white Swedish style

Preparation is very important for this technique; shortcuts may result in surface chipping if the crackle-glaze does not adhere. Strip any old wood panels and furniture with paint stripper, clean and sand them, prime with an all-purpose primer, and then sand again. All the paints used here are water-based so protect the finish with at least two coats of water-based polyurethane.

If the crackle-glazing is done neatly and carefully, the texturing can be a delight to look at, subtle and refined. Bold, obvious cracking is not necessarily the most attractive; smaller cracks displaying the deeper base color can be just as interesting and offer a more varied, realistic imitation of natural aging. Experiment with applications of thin and thick layers of crackle-glaze to decide the quality of cracking you wish to use.

YOU WILL NEED

For preparation
- White acrylic primer
- Fine-grade wet-and-dry sandpaper
- Pale blue flat latex paint

For waxing
- Beeswax

For painting
- Off-white, pale blue, and pink flat latex paint
- Crackle-glaze medium
- Low-luster water-based polyurethane
- Protective gloves
- Decorators' paintbrushes
- Artists' brush
- Paint buckets
- Steel wool
- Scraper
- Hair dryer
- Lint-free soft cloth or tack cloth

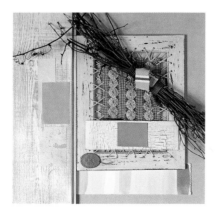

MOOD BOARD
Peeling paint, worn wood, and textured surfaces set against the typical colors and patterns of Scandinavian and New England fabrics offer a simple and relaxed melding of texture and pattern.

1 PREPARING THE SURFACE
Apply acrylic primer to all the woodwork, then lightly sand with fine-grade wet-and-dry sandpaper to achieve a smooth finish. Apply two coats of the blue base color carefully onto the tongue-and-groove paneling. Let it dry between coats.

2 APPLYING THE WAX

Using a paintbrush, apply beeswax randomly. Try to keep the waxed areas differently spaced and sized to give the worn and peeled patches a more natural appearance.

3 PAINTING

Paint over the base color and beeswax with the off-white latex paint. Cover well. Let dry using a hair dryer to help speed up the process.

4 Begin to lift off the top coat in the areas that have been waxed. Use a scraper and sandpaper and lightly rub over the surface to start the paint lifting.

5 Rub the whole surface with steel wool and polish and smooth the textured surface of the paint. This will deepen the off-white to a more worn and aged appearance.

6 Rub in some beeswax with fine steel wool as a protective layer. Buff to a gentle sheen with a soft cloth.

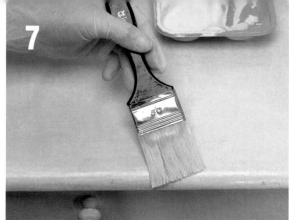

7 Prepare any furniture in the same way as the tongue-and-groove paneling. Apply the base color with a brush and paint two alternate coats of pink and pale blue. Let dry.

8 Apply the crackle-glaze medium liberally with a brush. Let dry.

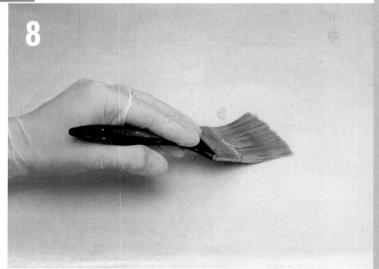

9 Use a paintbrush to apply the top coat in short, quick brush strokes. Do not overbrush the off-white because the crackle-glaze medium will be activated as soon as the topcoat has been applied. Let dry. Warm gently with a hair dryer to speed up the drying process.

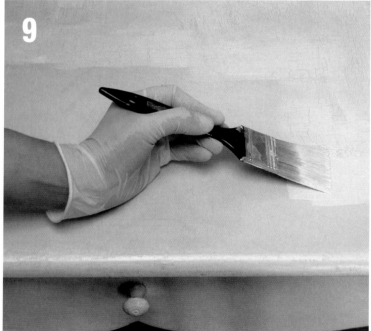

10 Lightly sand all over to give a smooth finish.

11 **FINISHING**
Using an artists' brush, add lining details in the blue and pink paint over the off-white. Let dry completely, then seal with two coats of low-luster water-based polyurethane for protection.

A wall painted in a dark color, such as eggplant, will often absorb light rather than reflect it. Bring the color to life and introduce some interest with this tried-and-true method of adding a hint of texture and delicate broken color.

Eggplant frottage

The frottage effect is created by laying newspaper over a wet glaze so that the paper absorbs some of the glaze, causing the remaining glaze to collect and reflect the creases, folds, and lines of the paper. When the paper is removed, the resulting random markings have a broken crazed effect, similar to a crackle-glaze. For a delicate and subtle effect, keep the base color and the top coat close in tone. For more radical and obvious texturing, try using a dark base color with a much lighter color for the top coat.

A large-scale project such as the one seen here, requires two people to work together quickly before the glaze dries. This is necessary to avoid visible "seams" between glazed areas, which may obscure the finer lines of the frottage. The base color has been enhanced with a first glaze layer stippled lightly to give more variety to the surface. The two colors are similar in tone, but the top coat has more white added. A protective low-luster water-based polyurethane has been applied in two thin coats to exaggerate the marking.

YOU WILL NEED

For preparation
- Two tones of eggplant flat latex paint
- White latex paint
- Foam roller and tray
- Fine-grade wet-and-dry sandpaper

For glaze mix
- Acrylic matte glaze
- Protective gloves
- Decorators' paintbrushes
- Paint buckets
- Newspaper
- Rubber texturing pad
- Fine-grade wet-and-dry sandpaper
- Low-luster water-based polyurethane

MOOD BOARD
Paint both a textured object and a flat board with the same color to demonstrate the way color changes when texture is added. While a gilded painting focuses attention, here, the color of the floor can radically affect the overall look.

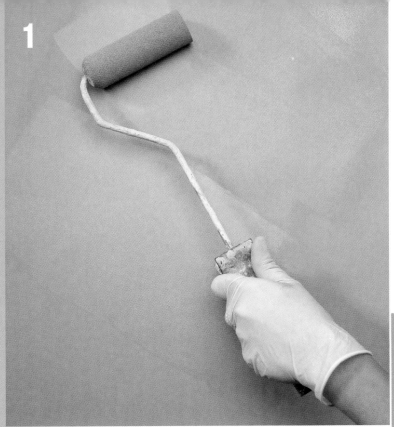

1 PREPARING THE SURFACE/APPLYING THE BASE COLOR

Decide on the two tones of eggplant paint. Mix the darker flat latex paint with some white latex paint in a 3:1 ratio, then mix the chosen top coat color with the same amount of acrylic matte glaze in a 1:1 ratio. This will make the paint more transparent and keep it fluid for longer. Using a roller, apply the first paint color, in as even a coverage as possible. Let dry.

2

When dry, lightly sand the surface with fine-grade wet-and-dry sandpaper. You need the surface to be as smooth as possible.

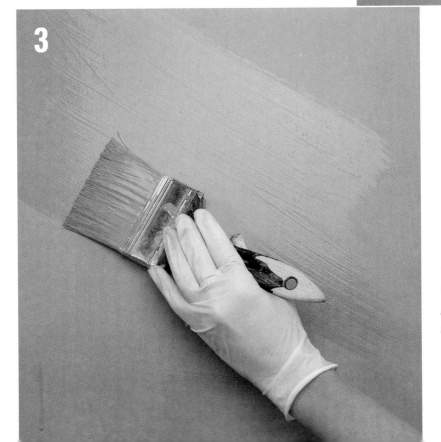

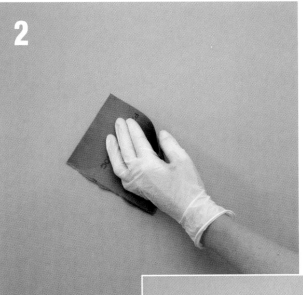

3 APPLYING THE GLAZE MIX

Mix the first paint color with acrylic matte glaze in a 2:1 ratio. Brush this over the area quickly in various directions to achieve an even coverage.

4 Quickly stipple the wet glaze with a rubber texturing pad to help even out the glaze and produce a slightly patterned look to the base color. Let dry thoroughly.

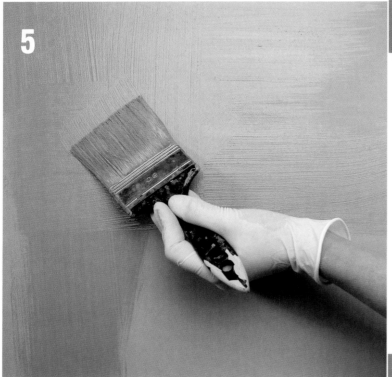

FROTTAGE TEXTURING

5 Dilute the whiter second coat with water in a 5:1 ratio. Prepare to begin the frottage texturing. It is best to open all the sheets of newspaper you think you will require and have them nearby. Work with your decorating partner from the top of the wall down. One person should apply the glaze and the other person should quickly lay the newspaper neatly over the wet area. It is best to work in sections so the glaze does not have time to dry before the paper is applied. Use a paintbrush and apply the glaze liberally and quickly.

6 Lay the sheets down quickly, butting up to the edges, and then rub the back smoothing the paper against the surface. The paper will begin to crinkle as it absorbs the glaze. As soon as the sheets have been held flat for a minute remove them carefully and quickly. Do not leave them for long because the ink will begin to adhere to the glaze. Let dry completely.

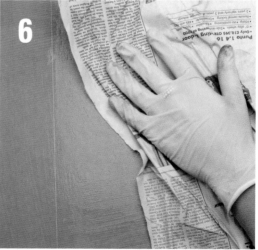

FINISHING

7 If you feel that some areas need more texture, repeat this step again, but work as fast as possible and be careful to rub the paper over the edges of each glazed area to avoid seams. Let dry, then lightly sand with fine-grade wet-and-dry sandpaper. Apply a coat of low-luster water-based polyurethane to protect the surface if you like.

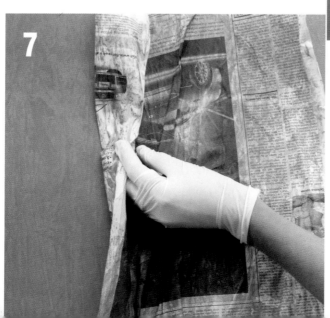

One-color schemes

The use of a paint effect can turn a one-color scheme from a flat painted wall into a work of art. Add some glamor with a silk moiré or marbling technique, or use tones of the same color to create sophisticated stripes.

◀ PINK MOIRÉ SILK EFFECT

Use a paintbrush to apply a midpink colorwash glaze over a pale pink base color in regular, vertical brush strokes. While the paint is still wet, pull a heart grainer through, starting from one end and working down in a regular, vertical direction. Pull slowly, and gently pivot the tool in a rocking motion to produce a wood grain effect. Drag a rubber comb through the wet glaze to create vertical stripes in some areas.

Soften the whole surface with a softening brush, following the direction of the previous brush strokes. Drag a flogging brush vertically over the surface, and then soften off again, this time against the direction of the grain. Let dry completely; then protect the finish with a coat of varnish.

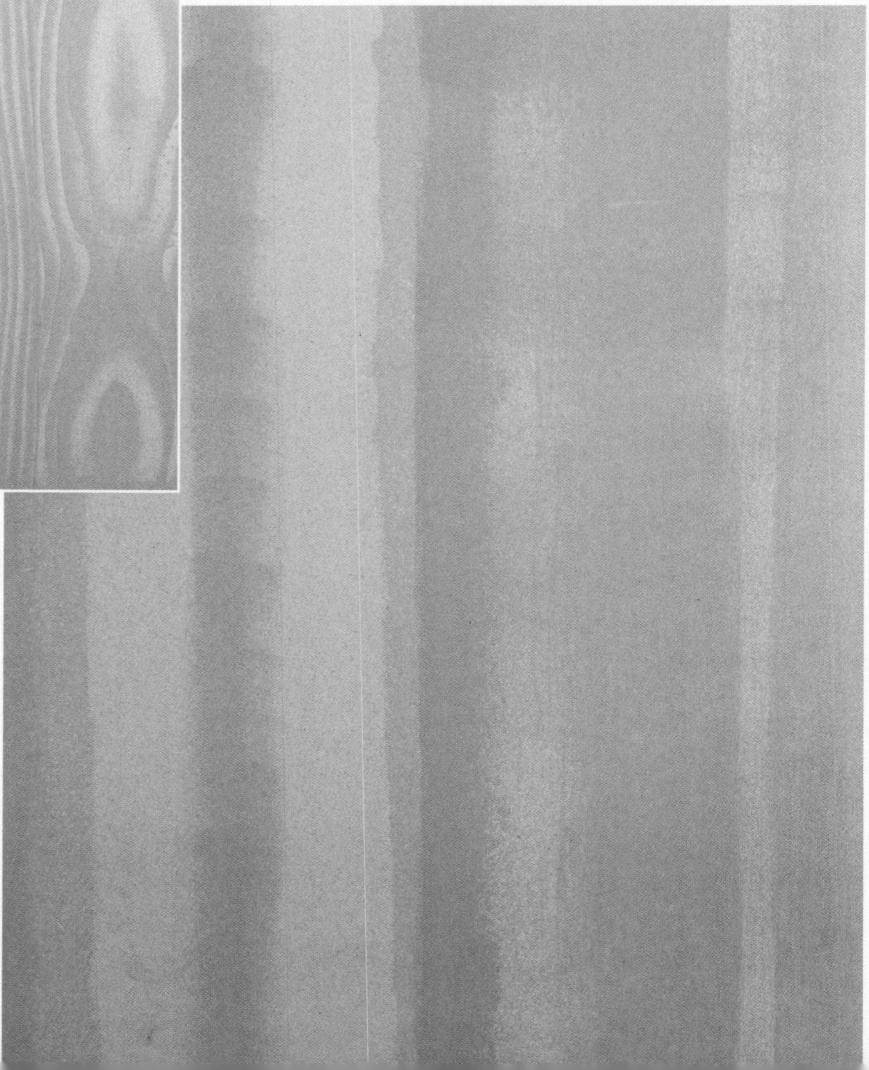

PINK AND LILAC STRIPES ▶

Use a large roller to create vertical stripes of broad bands of pink and lilac colors. Let dry. Apply thinner bands of other lighter and brighter pinks and lilac colors over the broad bands. Mix these lighter colors with matte glaze in a 2:1 ratio to render these top colors slightly transparent.

For a simple and natural effect, apply natural plaster, with no added colorants, to the surface in layers. As in the red and orange plaster effect scheme, polish the plaster to a shine. (See page 120.)

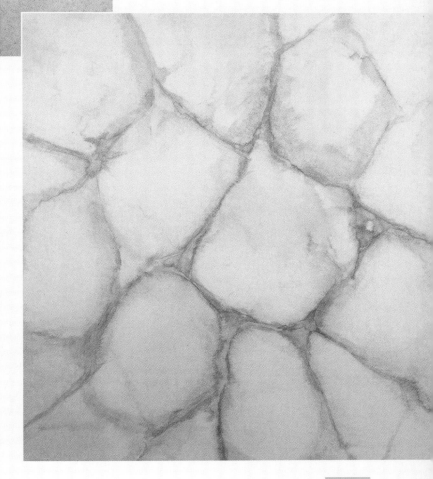

CREAM BRECCIA MARBLING ►

Apply two coats of white eggshell paint over the surface. Let dry, and lightly sand between coats with wet-and-dry sandpaper. Mix raw umber oil paint with liquid solvent in a 1:2 ratio, and brush a thin, even layer over the whole surface.

Use a lint-free cloth soaked in a little liquid solvent to wipe out areas of the glaze, and begin the pebble-like breccia marble pattern. Vary the size and look of the shapes: some should be small and angular; others should be large, round, and more pebble-like. Brush over in a variety of directions to blur the glaze edges. Let dry.

Use a long-haired sable brush and some raw umber oil paint mixed with just a touch of liquid solvent to paint the veining lines around the wiped-out shapes. Add a variety of subtle, lighter veining and others that are more graphic and darker in areas. Repeatedly blur the lines with light brush strokes from a softening brush, and wipe away those that appear too distinct with a soft cloth and a little liquid solvent. Let dry; then protect the finish with at least two coats of oil-based eggshell clear varnish.

CHAPTER 7 # Living with Pattern

INTRODUCE PATTERN TO UNIFY A SCHEME WITH STENCILING, STRIPES, AND PAINTED BANDS OF COLOR.

Interiors are often treated as a number of separate components, with the result that nothing quite fits together. Walls are left plain, and pattern and texture are invested only in the fabrics used for curtains and upholstery. Pictures and objects arranged around the room are the only figurative elements.

This chapter demonstrates how to unify all these components with some simple paint effects. Some delightful room schemes are created with the judicious use of pattern in harmonious color combinations. These combinations are found adjacent to each other on the color wheel—for example, green and yellow, blue and green, and red and orange. Such colors enhance each other and, however complex the pattern, blend easily together to produce a well-balanced effect.

A warm yellow color creates a relaxed and cosy environment—ideal for a lasting scheme in a child's bedroom. Liven up the ambiance with leaves stenciled in a random pattern throughout the room.

Green leaf stencil over pale yellow

Decorating a child's bedroom can be difficult. You don't want to go to a lot of trouble and expense to produce a scheme that the child may want to change later. Choosing the right colors is the key to an attractive, timeless design. Fresh, mood-enhancing colors, such as yellow and green, will create a relaxed and friendly atmosphere that will be popular for many years. Yellow is a warm, cheerful, unisex choice. The decorative detail of the green stenciled leaves is simple and interesting without appearing too childish.

The texture of the colorwashed walls suggests the dappling of sunlight through the window onto the walls, with areas of deeper cadmium yellow here and there. The two colors blend well in the room, retaining the cosy atmosphere.

YOU WILL NEED

For preparation
- Beige flat latex paint
- Foam roller and tray
- Deep cadmium yellow acrylic paint
- Green acrylic paint
- Cadmium yellow and white paint mix
- Acrylic matte glaze
- Protective gloves
- Decorators' paintbrushes
- Paint buckets

For stenciling
- Pencil
- Black marker
- Stencil paper or acetate
- Plain paper
- Tracing paper
- Craft knife
- Mat board
- Steel ruler
- Stencil brush
- Painters' tape

MOOD BOARD

A simple children's book illustration is the starting point for this scheme. A collection of leaves and different color swatches are brought together to produce the final effect.

1 PREPARING THE SURFACE

Apply two coats of beige latex paint to the walls with a roller. Use a paintbrush to stipple the corners. Dilute some deep cadmium yellow acrylic paint with water in a 2:1 ratio and, using a paintbrush, go over the walls in a cross-hatched pattern. This will give a random, uneven colorwash, with areas of dark and light yellow.

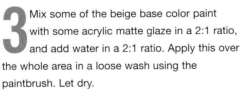

2 COLORWASH

Dilute some deep cadmium yellow and white paint mix with water in a 2:1 ratio and, using the same technique as in Step 1, apply a layer of pale yellow, overlapping with the dark yellow and filling the areas left beige. Let dry.

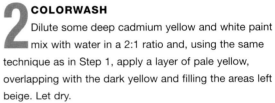

3

Mix some of the beige base color paint with some acrylic matte glaze in a 2:1 ratio, and add water in a 2:1 ratio. Apply this over the whole area in a loose wash using the paintbrush. Let dry.

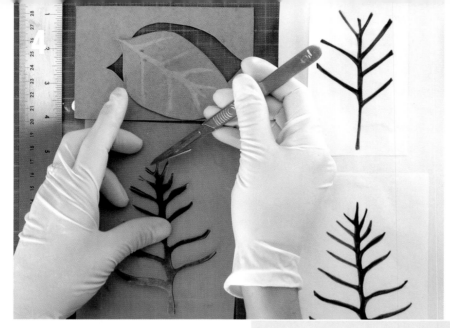

4 STENCILING

Using a pencil, draw some simple leaf designs on plain paper, then draw some simple leaf-vein details to stencil over the leaves. Fill in the designs with a black marker pen. You can photocopy the designs onto acetate or stencil paper, or trace and transfer to the stencil paper. Cut out using a sharp craft knife. Always cut the corners first to avoid any overcutting. Use a mat board and steel ruler to guide the knife.

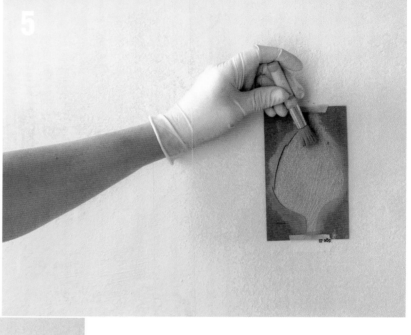

5 Consider where you wish to place the stencils and tape the first in position on the wall. Apply the color with a stencil brush, which has been dipped lightly in the chosen color. Let dry.

6 Place the second stencil over the leaf design already on the wall and use a slightly different green paint to add the veining. Use a small stencil brush again. Do not overload the brush.

Create dramatic effects in a space with a confident use of pattern. Using pastel colors in a design of simple stripes is a great way to add character and also has the effect of enlarging a small area—perfect for a kitchen or hallway.

Green and blue stripes

Introducing strong graphic decoration is a bold way to bring character and interest to a room. The simple, cartoon-like elements of the horizontal stripes and checkered floor suggest a fun and stimulating space. The colors are similar in tone and the combination has no dominant feature. Tinting the greens and blues with white creates an expansive look and has the effect of enlarging a small space. The strong, simple design offsets the traditional, restful, feminine feeling of pastel colors and adds zest to a neglected area, such as a hallway or stairwell. This decoration would also work well in a kitchen to give energy and fun to a strictly functional space.

YOU WILL NEED

For preparation
- White flat latex paint
- Medium-grade wet-and-dry sandpaper
- Roller and tray

For painting
- Five colors of flat latex paint in similar tones of blue and green
- Low-luster water-based polyurethane
- Protective gloves
- Decorators' paintbrushes
- Paint buckets
- Plumb line
- Pencil
- Ruler
- Painters' tape
- Fine-grade wet-and-dry sandpaper

MOOD BOARD
Strips of landscape photographs and paint chips have inspired this choice of colors. The effect is also influenced by the simplicity seen in cartoon painting and children's book illustrations.

1 PREPARING THE SURFACE

Apply at least two coats of white flat latex paint to the surface with a roller. Let dry. Lightly sand between coats to give a smooth finish. Drop a plumb line to assess if the walls are level and to find vertical lines to begin measuring the different widths of each required band around the walls. Use either a length of string marked with pencil marks at regular intervals or a straight edge with notches to measure and mark a series of different-sized stripes going horizontally around the walls.

2 PAINTING

Use masking tape to mask along the horizontal pencil lines to begin painting the first color. Paint the first stripe blue, using a paintbrush.

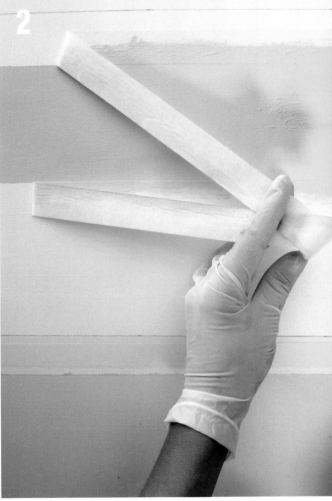

3

Move the tape to the new position ready to paint the next colors.

4 Paint the next color, a green stripe, and let dry.

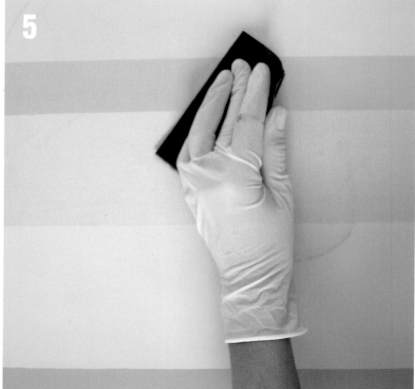

5 Repeat as in the previous steps until you have painted all the bands. Some bands may be thin and act as a highlight to the broader bands of color. The baseboard has also been decorated in a flat oil-based paint in a similar color to one of the wall colors.

6 FINISHING
When you are happy with the wall decoration, lightly sand the surface, then protect it with at least two coats of low-luster water-based polyurethane.

LIVING WITH PATTERN

Polished plaster is a fairly new and innovative product for home decorating and is used here to give interest to a room. Bands or stripes of shiny colored plaster are applied to a wall adding an extra dimension to the overall scheme.

Red and orange plaster effect

Polished plaster is introduced here to demystify specialist plastering for home decorators and to encourage experimentation with a relatively recent, readily available product. Don't avoid polished plaster; it can result in wonderful effects. The product used here is known as marmorino, which is a medium granulated lime and marble plaster dust.

Use this project as a guideline only; experimenting with plaster is essential to experience its full potential. Try adding different pigments and colorants for a variety of results. Lime-compatible pigments work best; the suggested range of earth colors or natural colorants offers a vast array of options. The process involved in building up the layers and the polishing of the plaster can be rather time-consuming but is ultimately very rewarding.

YOU WILL NEED

For preparation
- Acrylic primer
- Beige flat latex paint
- Foam roller and tray (two)
- Steel ruler
- Pencil

For plastering
- Dry-mix marmorino plaster with marble dust "key coat"
- Lime-compatible pigments in red and orange
- Acrylic glaze mix
- Protective gloves
- Goggles and face mask
- Electric drill with clutch control and mixing rod
- Mixing sticks or fitch paintbrushes
- Plasterers' hawk
- Stainless steel trowel
- Decorators' paintbrushes
- Cellulose decorators' sponges
- Paint buckets
- Painters' tape
- Beeswax
- Lint-free soft cloth or tack cloth

MOOD BOARD

Bands of minerals and sediment held in layers show a wonderful range of natural earth and mineral colors. The polished surface of certain samples has inspired the experiments with the lime-based marble dust plaster effect.

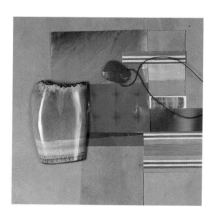

1 PREPARING THE SURFACE

Apply a coat of acrylic primer to the surface with a roller. When dry, apply some beige flat latex paint to the surface using another roller. Make sure that the surface is flat and without bumps, holes, or hollows. It is best to work with very good lighting and in a clean, warm environment. Use a steel ruler and pencil to measure and mark the scale of the stripes you wish to plaster.

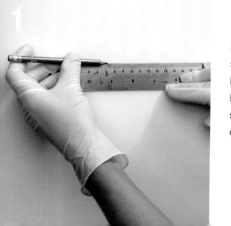

2 MARKING THE STRIPES

Using painters' tape, mask the edges of each alternate stripe ready to plaster. Make sure the tape is firmly in position so plaster cannot seep under the tape.

3 PLASTERING

Mix the dry plaster with water according to the manufacturer's guidelines. Make sure that you wear protective gloves, goggles, and a face mask. Stir the plaster into the water slowly, then use the drill and mixing rod to stir the mixture until a smooth, lump-free consistency is reached. Leave for 5 minutes, then whisk again before use.

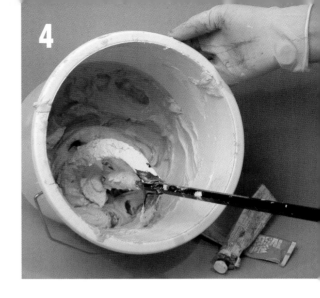

4 Divide the plaster into two batches. Mix again, adding the colorants to the batches of plaster. Only mix enough to use each day and keep a record of the quantities of colorant needed. Most pigments can be obtained in liquid suspension.

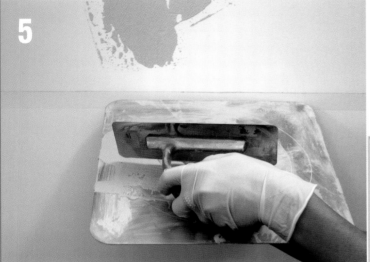

5 Scoop the mix onto a plasterers' hawk and practice using the hawk and trowel before applying the plaster. Try not to overload the hawk or trowel. Leave the plaster mix in a bucket with a damp cloth over it to keep out any dust and retain the moisture.

6 APPLYING THE PLASTER

Apply the plaster with the trowel over the area. Try to keep an even thickness. Lean the trowel at a 45-deg. angle to pull the plaster over the surface. Leave to semidry.

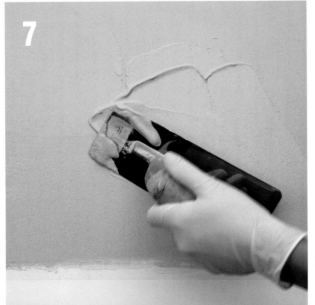

7 When the first coat is starting to dry and is no longer tacky to the touch, proceed with the next coat of colored plaster. Trowel in all directions to achieve a consistent coat. Add another layer when the second coat is touch dry. The third coat can be polished as it is applied. You can also polish this layer as it is nearly dry. Hold the trowel against the surface and pull in various directions at an almost vertical angle. Press firmly and pull steadily so you can feel the surface become smooth and shiny.

RED & ORANGE PLASTER EFFECT

8

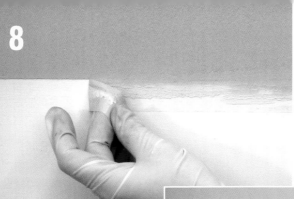

8 Unmask the edges of the first color, and then mask the dry plaster. Follow the same procedure to apply the second color. Keep checking that the tape has not lifted.

9 Completely remove the masking tape and polish both colored areas repeatedly. Try to polish the seams of the bands of color, because the plaster often builds up at the edge of the tape.

9

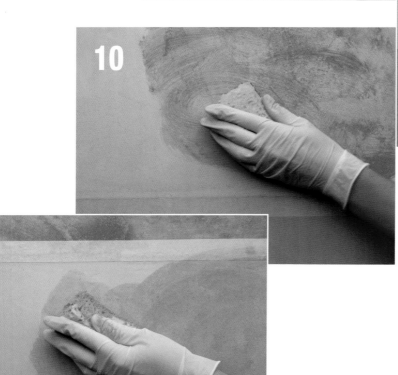

10

10 You can enhance the color of the plaster by washing with a mix of colorant and acrylic glaze in a 2:1 ratio. The absorbency of the plaster is affected by the polishing, so the color must be applied slowly with a repeated circular motion using a sponge to allow time for the color to be absorbed. Make sure you tape very carefully along the edge of each band and check the adhesion of the tape regularly.

11 FINISHING
When the color is completely dry, add a protective layer of beeswax applied with a soft cloth, then buff to a sheen.

11

Pattern

Treat your scheme as a whole by unifying it with the use of rich detail and pattern. The possibilities offered by pattern are endless; these are just a few suggestions.

◄ TONGUE-AND-GROOVE PANELING WITH GREEN CRACKLE GLAZE

This variation is similar to the crackled poppy red and spring green scheme. (See page 52.) Apply a blue-green base color all over the tongue-and-groove paneling. Let dry, then apply a crackle glaze medium followed by a darker green paint. Let dry. Wash some blue acrylic paint over alternate wood panels with a paintbrush. When this is completely dry, apply alternate top coat layers of green and blue opalescent paints over the paneling to finish the effect.

STENCILED ORANGE AND RED SQUARES ►

Measure and mark out the stencil to the size you wish to use; then cut it out. Measure and mark the positions of the stencil over the surface to be decorated. Fix the stencil to the surface with masking tape.

Use a damp sponge and some red flat latex paint to stipple repeatedly through the stencil over alternate squares. Move the stencil when the paint is dry. Repeat with the orange color over the other squares. Let dry.

Using a damp sponge, stipple a top coat of red glitter paint on the red squares and a coat of orange opalescent paint on the alternate orange squares. These opalescent paints will add a protective sealant coat.

◄ MULTICOLORED STRIPES

Measure and mark out each stripe with a straightedge and pencil. Paint each color in flat latex paint. Use masking tape to help paint the straight edges: tape the edges of alternate colors, and remove and re-tape as each color is dry.

MULTICOLORED SPOTS ►

Use a sponge to apply a coat of cream latex paint over a cream base color, and build up the layers until you achieve a solid base of color.

Dab the end of a fine foam radiator roller head into various latex paint colors. Dab off the excess and lightly press the paint-loaded end onto the surface and remove.

Continue to create a random pattern of spots. Let dry. Use a small fitch brush to paint central dots of acrylic metallic paint in various colors. Let dry. Sand the pattern lightly to give a smooth finish, and seal the finish with a matte acrylic glaze.

Glossary

ACRYLIC PAINT Fast-drying water-based paints.

AGING Variety of techniques for simulating the effect of time and wear on a surface.

BASE COAT First coat of paint for most decorative paint finishes.

BORDER Design around the edge of panel, wall, floor, etc.

BUFF Polish with a cloth.

COLORWASHING Water-based paint technique. Several layers of thin paint are applied to produce a softly-textured, patchy finish.

COMBING Technique in which a decorators' comb is scraped through a surface glaze to reveal the color below.

COMPLEMENTARY COLORS Any pair of colors in opposing positions on a color wheel.

CRACKLE GLAZE Decorative glaze that produces a fine network of cracks. (Also known as *craquelure*.)

CROSS-HATCHING Two sets of parallel lines, one on top of the other, with the second set at an angle to the first.

DISTEMPER Paints formed by mixing pigments with water, bound with casein, glue, or egg. Widely used before the introduction of latex paints.

DISTRESSING Process of artificially abrading a new surface to create the appearance of age.

DRAGGING Technique of pulling a long-haired brush through wet transparent oil glaze or distemper to produce a series of fine lines.

DRY-BRUSHING Using brush bristles relatively dry in order to build up a cloudy effect or to touch up the highlights of a textured surface.

EGGSHELL Midsheen oil- or acrylic-based paint used as a base coat. Also describes a midsheen finish of paints and varnishes.

EMULSION *See latex.*

FAUX EFFECTS Literally: "false" effects or finishes created to imitate another material, such as marble or wood.

FITCH Hog hair brush which can be used as an alternative to a household brush.

FLAT FINISH Matte, non-glossy finish.

FLOGGING Technique in which colored glaze is laid over a base coat, then flogged with a long-bristled brush to give a mottled effect.

FLOGGING BRUSH Coarse horsehair brush used for dragging and flogging.

FROTTAGE Literally: "rubbing." Technique involving rubbing newsprint over a wet glaze.

GESSO Fine plaster traditionally prepared with glue and whiting, and applied in many layers to give a completely smooth finish before gilding or painting.

GILDING An application of metal leaf or paint for a metallic finish.

GLAZE Transparent mixture of linseed oil, driers, whiting, and other oils in which color is mixed. Water-based glazes are also available.

HEART GRAINER Comb that produces faux wood-grain effects.

HOG HAIR BRUSH Tough and springy, suitable for acrylic- and oil-painting.

HUE The specific spectral name of a color, such as red, yellow, or blue. Pink, for example, is a red hue.

LACQUERING Technique for simulating the high-gloss finish of Chinese and Japanese lacquer.

LATEX *See also emulsion.* Water-based paint.

LIMEWASH *See also whitewash.* Mix of slaked lime and water used for whitening exterior walls.

LINING PAPER Plain, flat wallpaper used to line walls, often over imperfect plaster.

MARMORINO PLASTER A medium granulated lime and marble plaster dust.

MASKING Covering a surface to provide a barrier against a layer of paint.

MASKING TAPE Used to mask out areas, hold on stencils, etc.

METHYLATED SPIRITS Industrial alcohol used as a solvent.

MICA Rock-forming mineral, such as slate, which crystallizes into easily-separated layers.

OXIDATION Chemical reaction of a material with oxygen.

PATINA Color and texture that appear on the surface of a material as a result of age or atmospheric corrosion.

PATINATION Artificial patina.

PIGMENT Coloring matter used in paints.

PLUMB LINE Weighted string used for marking vertical lines.

PRIMARY COLORS Colors from which all others can be mixed: the primary colors of pigment are red, yellow, and blue.

PRIMER Sealant for new plaster or woodwork before painting.

RAGGING Broken-color finish created using a crumpled rag.

ROLLER Tool with a revolving cylinder used for applying paint.

SANDPAPER Abrasive paper available in various grades. *See wet-and-dry sandpaper.*

SCUMBLE *See glaze.*

SECONDARY COLORS Colors made by mixing two primary colors.

SOFTENING BRUSH Long-haired brush (either badger- or hog hair) used for softening and blending paint in marbling, wood-graining, and other finishes.

SOLVENT Part of oil-based paints that evaporates during drying.

SPONGING Paint technique that uses a damp sponge to produce a mottled, patchy effect.

SPRAYING Directing paint onto a surface in a fine spray.

STAINERS *See tinter.* Also known as universal stainers. Used as an alternative to artists' oil colors for coloring glaze. The range of colors is less extensive and less subtle than artists' oils.

STENCIL BRUSH Short-haired brushes designed to hold small amounts of paint for stenciling.

STENCIL PAPER Stout, oiled cardstock or thick cartridge paper, from which shapes are cut.

STENCILING The application of paint through a cut-out design to create images on a surface.

STIPPLING Painting a surface with a fine, mottled pattern.

STIPPLING BRUSH Rectangular brush used for a stippled finish and for removing excess paint in cornices and architraves, etc.

STUCCO Fine plaster-type material used to cover exterior brickwork and to decorate interior walls and ceilings.

TERTIARY COLORS Colors made by mixing two secondary colors.

TINTER *See stainer.* Highly concentrated coloring agent. Also known as universal tinter.

TONE Term used to describe how dark or light a color is. Different colors may be the same tone.

TONGUE-AND-GROOVE Joint made when a tongue projecting from the edge of one board slots into a groove along the edge of another.

UNDERCOAT Flat paint applied to a surface before the base coat.

VARNISH Transparent protective coat applied to completed paint finishes.

WET-AND-DRY SANDPAPER Abrasive paper that may be used with water to achieve a really smooth finish.

WHITEWASH *See limewash.*

WHITING Finely ground calcium carbonate used in making gesso.

WOOD-GRAINING Technique used to imitate the characteristic markings of a variety of natural wood-grains.

Index

A
acrylic paint 11, 126
acrylic primer 10
acrylic thinners 12
acrylic water-based
  polyurethane 12
aging 36-8, 126
artists' oil paints 11

B
base coat 126
beeswax 12
bold color 15-29
border 126
bronze powder 12
buff 126

C
cardstock 13
color
  definition 8
  theory 6-7
color wheel 7
colored wax 12
colorwashing 11, 20-2, 29, 32-4,
  44, 45, 48-50, 72-4, 76, 77, 126
combining colors 47-61, 126
complementary colors 8,
  60-1, 126
cool colors 8
crackle glaze 52-4, 100-2,
  124, 126
craft knife 13
cross-hatching 126

D
decorators' paintbrushes 10
distemper 126
distressing 126
dragging 126
dragging brushes 11
dry-brushing 126

E
eggshell 11, 126
emulsion 126

F
fading 36-8
faux effects 56-8, 64-6,
  80-90, 126
fillers 12

finishes 12
fitch 126
fitch brushes 11
flat finish 126
flogging 126
flogging brush 126
frottage 104-6, 126

G
geometric panels 96-8
gesso 126
gilding 126
glaze 126

H
harmonious colors 7
health and safety 12
heart grainer 126
heart graining tools 13
hog hair brush 126
hue 8, 126

I
intensity 8

L
lacquering 16-18, 126
latex 126
latex paint 11
layering colors 31-43
light effects and texture 9
limewash 126
liming wax 12
lint-free cloth 13

M
marbling 109
marmorino plaster 44, 126
masking 126
masking tape 13, 126
matte latex varnish 12
metal patina 92
metallic paint 11
metallic powder 12
methylated spirits 126
mica 126
mixed and muted colors 63-77
moiré effect 108
monochromatic style 8, 95-109
mood colors 9

N
natural color and texture 79-93
neutral color combinations 8

O
oil-based paint 11
oil-based primer 10
oil-based thinners 12
oil-based varnish 12
one-color schemes *see*
  monochromatic effect
opalescent shimmer powder 12
oxidation 126

P
paints 10-11
paneling 124
patina 126
patination 126
patterns 111-24
pencil, eraser, chalk 13
plaster 11, 28, 32-4, 56-8
plaster effect 93, 109, 120-2
plasterers' hawk and float 13
plastic containers 13
plumb line 13, 126
powders 12
primary colors 7, 28-9, 126
primer 10, 126

R
ragging 126
real bristle nailbrushes 11
resin-based water-soluble
  varnish 12
roller 10, 126
ruler, steel ruler, straightedge,
  measuring tape 13
rusted iron effect 80-2

S
sandpaper 13, 126
scalpel 13
scissors 13
scrapers 13
scumble *see glaze*
secondary colors 7, 44-5, 126
softening brush 11, 126
solvent 126
spirit level 13
sponges 10
sponging 126

spots 61, 125
spraying 126
stainers 126
stencil brush 11, 126
stencil paper 13, 126
stenciling 60, 112-14, 124, 126
stippling 45, 126
stippling brush 126
stone block effect 92
stone effect 88-90, 92
stripes 108, 116-18, 125
stucco 28, 44, 126
suede effect 86
Swedish style 100-2

T
tertiary colors 7, 76-7, 126
textured paints 11
thinners 12
tile effect 56-8
tinter *see stainer*
tone 126
tongue-and-groove 100-2,
  124, 126
tools and equipment 10-13
transparent oil glaze 12

U
undercoat 10, 126

V
value 8
varnish 12, 126
varnishing brushes 11
verdigris 68-70, 77

W
warm colors 8
washes *see colorwashing*
water-based thinners 12
waxes 12
weathering 40-2
wet-and-dry sandpaper 126
whitewash *see limewash*
whiting 126
wire brushes 11
wire wool 13
wood paint 11
wood-graining 64-6, 126

Acknowledgments

This book is dedicated to my father, Christopher John Skinner OBE.
We all miss you every day.

Particular thanks to my extended family and supporters: Stephen, Jessie,
Heather, Jack, Martin, Rob, and Lynne, Ana, Noah, Simon, Holly, J.P., Zibi, and
the Grace and Skinner families during a difficult and testing 18 months.
Thank you to Piers Ostroumoff and Zibi Kopyto for their patience and hard work with the
studio and set building. A special mention for Sarah Davis, a rare talent and inspiration:
thank you for your unique support and assistance throughout this project.
Thank you to Tim France for the wonderful photographs, and the hours of work
and fun—good luck with your travels.
Thanks to Leyland SDM, London, and Kirby and Garton, Bath for paints and equipment.
Thank you to Piers Spence, Moira Clinch, Kate Kirby, and Jo Fisher at Quarto for your
trust and support in continuing to produce quality books together.

The stone effect fire surround scheme features a painting by Tracey Perrett.
The poppy red and spring green crackle-glaze scheme features a painting
by Mary Matheson.
Picture on page 6 Narratives / Jan Baldwin.

Metric conversion table

Volume

1 cubic inch	$16.3870cm^3$		
1 cubic foot	$0.03m^3$		
1 cubic yard	$0.77m^3$		

Capacity

1 fluid ounce	29.57ml
1 pint	473.18ml
1 quart	1.14l
1 gallon	3.79l

Weight

1 ounce	28.35g
1 pound	0.45kg

Area

1 square inch	$645mm^2$
1 square foot	$929cm^2$
1 square yard	$0.8361m^2$
1 acre	$404.86m^2$
1 square mile	$2.59km^2$

Length

1 inch	25.4mm
1 foot	30.48cm
1 yard	0.9144m
1 mile	1.61km